# *Marvel Studios' Avengers: Endgame*

Based on the Screenplay by
Christopher Markus and Stephen McFeely
Story by Stan Lee and Jack Kirby

Produced by Kevin Feige, p.g.a.
Directed by Anthony and Joe Russo

## Level 5

Retold by Lynda Edwards

Series Editors: Andy Hopkins and Jocelyn Potter

**Pearson Education Limited**
KAO Two
KAO Park, Harlow,
Essex, CM17 9NA, England
and Associated Companies throughout the world.

ISBN: 978-1-2923-4751-6
This edition first published by Pearson Education Ltd 2018
1 3 5 7 9 10 8 6 4 2

Set in 9pt/14pt Xenois Slab Pro
Printed by Neografia, Slovakia

Published by Pearson Education Limited

For a complete list of the titles available in the Pearson English Readers series, visit
**www.pearsonenglishreaders.com.**
Alternatively, write to your local Pearson Education office or
to Pearson English Readers Marketing Department,
Pearson Education, KAO Two, KAO Park, Harlow, Essex, CM17 9NA

# Contents

# Who's Who?

### Thanos

Thanos, born on the planet Titan, is a cruel, violent warlord with superhuman strength and abilities. To solve problems of overpopulation in the universe, he destroyed half of all living things. His assistant, **Ebony Maw**, is a skilled magician.

### Steve Rogers / Captain America

Rogers was given superpowers by the U.S. government, became Captain America, and fell in love with **Peggy Carter**. After a heroic plane crash in the Arctic, he was unconscious for sixty-six years before becoming an Avenger.

### Natasha Romanoff / Black Widow

Natasha was trained by the Russian security service as a spy and highly effective killer. She was later persuaded to join the U.S. agency S.H.I.E.L.D., and is now—as Black Widow—an extremely skillful fighter for the Avengers.

### Tony Stark / Iron Man

Stark is a smart, wealthy scientist and inventor. He developed a special suit that gives him superhuman strength and powers as Iron Man in his fights with the Avengers team. Stark and his wife, **Pepper Potts**, have a young daughter, **Morgan**.

### Bruce Banner / Hulk

Banner is a smart scientist who, as the result of a laboratory accident, becomes Hulk—an enormous, violent, green-skinned creature—when he is angry. He isn't always an enthusiastic Avenger.

### Scott Lang / Ant-Man

As Ant-Man, Lang can become tiny or enormous. He has been in the Quantum Realm, knowing nothing of events on Earth, on a journey controlled by his girlfriend, **Hope van Dyne**.

### Clint Barton / Hawkeye

Barton was a S.H.I.E.L.D. agent before joining the Avengers. As Hawkeye, he has no superpowers, but is extremely skilled with a bow and arrows. Now retired, he lives with his wife and children.

### James "Rhodey" Rhodes / War Machine

Rhodes was a U.S. Air Force officer when he met his close friend, Tony Stark. Stark made his War Machine suit, which he has worn to help the Avengers.

### Nebula

Nebula and her dead sister, **Gamora**—who she loved and hated—were kidnapped and adopted by Thanos, and trained to be killers. She has been helping the Avengers in their fight with Thanos.

### Rocket

Rocket is a scientifically improved engineer who builds powerful weapons. **Peter Quill/Star-Lord**, **Drax**, **Mantis**, and **Groot**—the other Guardians of the Galaxy—have disappeared.

### Thor

Thor, God of Thunder, was King of Asgard. He uses lightning to control his magical weapons—Mjolnir, the hammer, and Stormbreaker, the ax. With superhuman strength, he helps the Avengers.

### Valkyrie

Valkyrie was one of a group of Asgardian fighters defeated by Thor's evil sister, Hela. She moved to Sakaar, but has lived on Earth with other Asgardians since the destruction of their planet.

### Carol Danvers / Captain Marvel

Danvers becomes Captain Marvel, a hero with great strength and the ability to fly through space without the need for a spaceship. She helps anyone in the universe who needs it.

### Dr. Stephen Strange / Doctor Strange

Before his disappearance, Strange was trained by **the Ancient One**, a very powerful sorcerer, to protect Earth against dangerous, magical powers. He was helped by his assistant, **Wong**.

### T'Challa / Black Panther

Before he disappeared, T'Challa was King of Wakanda. His superpowers gave him the abilities of a big cat. His sister, **Shuri**, was a scientist. **Okoye** was the head of the Wakandan guards.

### Other Avengers

Among the "disappeared" are also **Wanda Maximoff/Scarlet Witch**, **"Bucky" Barnes/Winter Soldier**, **Peter Parker/Spider-Man**, and **Sam Wilson/Falcon**—and **Nick Fury**, who created the Avengers.

# Introduction

*"See you in a minute," Natasha said to Rogers. The tunnel became active with a roaring noise, like the sound of a jet plane, and a spinning light show of flashing red and gold. The platform fell away, and the Avengers disappeared into the pulsing mouth below. Each team was racing through different twisted tunnels at speeds much greater than anything they could ever have imagined.*

After a desperate fight to prevent Thanos from finding all six Infinity Stones and using them to destroy half of all living things in the universe, the Avengers and their friends lose the final battle and watch as many of the people they love become dust. It appears that the moment that Thanos snapped his fingers while wearing the Infinity Gauntlet cannot be changed. But is that true? Can those who remain discover a way to bring back "the disappeared?"

The series of exciting Marvel Studios' movies has brought people unforgettable heroes from Captain America to Ant-Man, from Black Widow to Black Panther, taking them from Earth to distant planets. Humans, gods, and creatures from many other planets have featured in films showing the battles between the forces of good and evil. *Marvel Studios' Avengers: Infinity War*, which came out in 2018, brought Avengers, Guardians of the Galaxy, and other heroes together in the first part of the two-part final story of The Infinity Saga. *Marvel Studios' Avengers: Endgame* (2019) gives us the ending in an electrifying story of the battle for good.

The Infinity Stones have featured in previous Marvel Studios films, and are Stones with different powers that can be used, or held, by only a few because of their enormous power.

The red **Reality Stone** can change reality.

The green **Time Stone** allows its user to make time go backward or forward.

The blue **Space Stone** is hidden inside a container called the Tesseract. Its user can travel through portals to different parts of the universe.

The purple **Power Stone** gives its user enormous energy to create or destroy.

The yellow **Mind Stone** can be used to control the minds of others.

The orange **Soul Stone** allows its user to control people's souls and gives the user control over all life in the universe.

Brought together, they can cause change and destruction on an unimaginable level, but Thanos's search for all the Stones was a difficult and dangerous one. He succeeded, and in *Avengers: Endgame* we see the results of what he could achieve with them. *Avengers: Endgame* follows the story of how the few brave remaining heroes try to regain the Stones—and how much it costs them.

A previous story in the Marvel Studios' movies has been the discovery and use of the Quantum Realm, which is a universe with different rules about time and space. The scientist Hank Pym discovered that it was possible to go into this universe by becoming subatomic, and Pym Particles allow people and objects to do this. In *Marvel Studios' Ant-Man and The Wasp* (2018), we learn a great deal about the importance of the Quantum Realm, and it is of great importance in *Avengers: Endgame*, too.

Also important to the stories is the problem of overpopulation. The increase in population has created problems for our planet that people in every country have to face today, and these stories show and consider Thanos's solution in relation to a whole fictional universe.

In the title, the word "endgame" suggests that we are going to read about the final stage of a very long battle. The word is usually used when we come to the last moves in a game or a competition—the moves that will decide the winner. *Avengers: Endgame* gives us a winner. Is it the side that we expect to win, or not?

# Barton Farm, Missouri

Lila feels the warmth and strength of her father's hand on her shoulders as he gently corrects her position. His foot pushes against hers slightly to point it in the right direction. She raises the bow.

"Can you see where you're aiming?"

"Yes, Dad." Lila tries to concentrate on her target, a round board on a tree.

"And now?" Clint Barton pulls some of her dark hair to cover one of her eyes. "Can you see now?"

They laugh, and he stands back as she raises the bow again. In the distance, she can hear her brothers playing a ball game. Her mother is setting out a picnic in the summer sunshine. It is another day on the farm, just one more day, no different from the ones before it. Sunshine, birdsong, sweet, still air, and grass and trees as far as they can see.

"I want ketchup on my hot dog," one of the boys shouts, and throws the ball. The air is so calm that Lila can hear the gentle *thud* as it is caught in his brother's baseball glove.

Lila points at the target and her eyes half close. She pulls back the arrow and feels the controlled energy in the tight string. The arrow trembles slightly between her fingers. Then, the air seems to grow stiller. Her brothers' voices have faded. Lila is caught in that special moment that she always experiences, when the world seems to be holding its breath.

Then.

She lets the arrow fly.

She closes her eyes and hears the faint whisper as it cuts through the air; the singing *thud* when it sinks into the board. Right in the center.

"Hey, Hawkeye!" Barton is proud of his daughter. Lila has his talent with the bow—a talent that made him, the *real* Hawkeye, a dangerous member of the Avengers team. He pulls the arrow from the target as his wife calls that lunch is ready.

"O.K. We're coming!" He turns back to Lila, but she isn't there.

"Lila?" Barton walks around the tree. No one. Then he looks across to the picnic table. The food is there, but only spaces where there had been people. Confused, he turns full circle. Then, he feels it—the faint *buzz* of a strange electricity on his skin. He stands quite still, and fear touches his heart. All around him is silence; the air has become dead. All sound and life have been swallowed up.

Clint Barton is completely alone.

# Death of a Titan

"You've won." Tony Stark stretched his hand across the table to congratulate Nebula. She had flicked the folded silver paper across his spread fingers to score the final "goal" in their game. Still unused to the way humans' minds worked, she looked, unsure, at Stark's hand. What should she do with it? She slowly placed her own hand in it to be shaken. Another new experience to be stored away inside her gray and blue head.

"It was fun," she said, quietly and unemotionally as always.

Stark moved to the front of the Guardians of the Galaxy spaceship, where he could look out into the silent emptiness of outer space. He sat on the floor with his Iron Man helmet in front of him and switched on its recording device. The eyes flashed blue. He leaned back, exhausted, and rested his head against the chair. The bright smile that he had worn during the game with Nebula had faded.

"Pepper." He was recording for the woman he loved. "If you ever get this message, do *not* post it on social media. It's going to be a bit too sad."

He looked out into the darkness. The spaceship was hanging in space like a great, dead bird. Broken, after the battle with Thanos, powerless and drifting. Stark and Nebula had gained some time by fixing the fuel cells, but now the last of the fuel was gone.

"I don't know if you'll get this. I don't know if you're even still ... but—I hope so ... The Blue Metal Lady closed my wounds and cured my infection, but there's no more food and little oxygen." His voice grew quieter. He knew he was going to die. "I wanted, I *hoped* for a last surprise. But ... there isn't one. But please—when I drift off, it will be fine, I promise you. I'll dream of you, as always. Because it's always you."

His voice became a whisper; he was so tired. Stark switched off the recording and lay back on the cold, metal floor. He put his head on his arm and kept the picture of Pepper in his mind for as long as he could. Then, he closed his eyes, his breathing slowed, and Tony Stark went to sleep.

Nebula found him later. She felt an unusual emotion as she gently touched his body and lifted him into the seat that looked out into space. She did not want his last moments to be on a hard floor. The stars shone silver blue on his cool cheeks.

And then, something changed. Slowly, a warm, orange light moved across Stark's face. It touched his eyelids, and they trembled. Automatically, his hand lifted to shield his face, and he opened his eyes. The light flooding in through the glass was impossibly bright, but he could see, or *thought* he could see, someone *outside* the ship. A woman.

In the mirror at the Avengers' base, Steve Rogers's face was tired. Lines showed the exhaustion of the last few weeks, and his eyes were dull with defeat. The strong features of Captain America, brave Avenger, were hardly recognizable. Then, his face started trembling. But it wasn't his face, it was the mirror. A low rumble filled the building; something heavy was thundering through the sky above it.

He ran outside to find his friends—Natasha Romanoff, Bruce Banner, James "Rhodey" Rhodes, and Pepper Potts, Tony Stark's partner—watching as a great, black spaceship moved through the dark sky. What *was* it? Who was *in* it? Rogers then realized something that seemed an impossibility, even to him. The great ship wasn't flying. It was being carried. Something enormously powerful, surrounded by shining gold energy, was gently bringing the ship safely down to the ground.

The gold energy faded, and Steve saw a young woman with blond hair. She gave a slight smile, and he recognized Carol Danvers, Captain Marvel. Then, his eyes fixed on a familiar figure coming down the steps from the ship. It was Tony Stark, but not the Stark he remembered. This Stark was a shadow of the strong, fearless leader of the Avengers. The man was thin and pale and could hardly put one foot in front of the other.

Rogers rushed to support his friend's weight.

"I couldn't stop him." Stark's voice was low and breathless, and Steve could only just hear his words. But he understood.

"Neither could I," he said, his voice a whisper, too.

Stark stopped, and Rogers saw that his eyes were wet. "I lost the kid." Stark's voice was breaking as he remembered the boy he had encouraged to be Spider-Man. "I lost Peter."

Rogers had no words of comfort. He slowly shook his head. "Tony," he said, "*we* lost."

"It's been twenty-three days since Thanos came to Earth, snapped his fingers, and destroyed half of all living creatures." Natasha's clear voice hid her emotions. "He did as he promised."

Holographic pictures of the Avengers' friends flashed on the screens around the meeting room: Wanda Maximoff, T'Challa, Hank Pym, Scott Lang, Peter Parker … and more, so many more. The word "missing" followed each one. Stark watched from a wheelchair. With each name that appeared on the screens, something died inside him. His normally clear head was a mess of confusion and anger and helplessness.

Rogers continued the story. "Afterward, Thanos opened a portal and walked through," he continued. "We have no idea where he is now."

"What's wrong with *him?*" Stark pointed at Thor.

The big man was sitting silent, locked in his own world. He was remembering Thanos's laugh after Thor had buried his ax in his chest. *You didn't attack the head!* The words would stay with him forever. He didn't attack the head. If he had, the Titan—Thanos was from the planet Titan—would be dead now, and Thor's friends would still be alive.

"He thinks he failed," Rocket, one of the Guardians of the Galaxy, explained. "And, of course, he did. But he's not the only one."

"We've looked for Thanos, Tony. But we can't find him," Rogers said. "You fought him. Can you give us any ideas? Any clues?"

Stark's face twisted in anger. "I *didn't* fight. He threw me around the planet like I was a ball. And then, that crazy sorcerer—Doctor Strange—gave him, *gave* him the Time Stone to save *my life.*" He was alive, but the cost was unimaginable.

"Tony, we need you ..."

"I needed *you!*" Suddenly, Stark couldn't control himself, and attacked his old friend. Each word was intended to hurt. "*We* needed you—and where *were* you?" Stark pointed accusingly at Rogers. "I told you—remember? I *told* you we needed a shield around Earth to keep us all safe, but—no—you wanted to protect our valuable "freedoms." I said we'd lose, and what did you say? You said, if we lose, we'll lose together." Anger was burning a tight band around his head. "And guess what, Cap? We lost!"

Stark pulled the Iron Man power source from his chest. What use was it? It had not prevented the greatest of all disasters. He fell on the floor, unconscious.

For a moment, the Avengers stared at him in stunned silence.

Then, Captain Marvel stepped forward. "Take care of him," she said calmly, and turned. "I'm going to kill Thanos."

"When Thanos snapped his fingers, there was an enormous explosion of energy, bigger than anything before."

Rogers followed her. "Space is more your world than ours, but this is our fight, too. We work as a team. And anyway, no one knows where he is."

"*I* do." Nebula's voice came from the shadows. "Thanos spent a long time trying to make me perfect, hurting me, remaking me piece by piece. I was part of his great plan. As he worked on me, I asked him where we would go when his plan was complete." She touched her metal cheek as she remembered the pain, and his promises. "His answer was always the same," she told them. "To the Garden."

"So Thanos has a retirement plan," Rhodey said quietly.

"Look!" Rocket pointed at two holograms. "When Thanos snapped his fingers, there was an enormous explosion of energy, bigger than anything before. And then, two days ago—on *this* planet ..." He pointed at the second hologram. "A second explosion."

"Thanos is there!" Nebula said. It was Planet 0259-S—known as the Garden—a planet owned by Thanos.

Natasha went pale. "He used the Stones again."

"We go, we find him, we use the Stones to bring everyone back," Carol said calmly.

Slowly, Thor stood up and moved to look the new member of the team in the eye. Something flashed in his own eyes, and he held out his empty hand, a call for his weapon. The air trembled, and Stormbreaker—his magic ax, created after he had lost his Asgardian weapon, Mjolnir—found its home. It passed so close to the woman's head that the wind from its speed flicked her hair, but she didn't move. The corner of her mouth raised in a smile.

Thor's eyes didn't leave hers. "I like you," he said.

Rogers looked around the room. "O.K.," he said. "Let's go get Thanos."

"Hands up who has never been to space before." Rocket looked around at his passengers on the spaceship.

Black Widow, War Machine, and Captain America cautiously raised their hands. As the spaceship had lifted off in a violent burst of power, their stomachs had lifted with it, and then dropped.

Rocket laughed. "Just don't be sick in my spaceship!" He pushed the ship faster and faster toward the space jump point.

"Space jump—in three–two–one ..." Nebula counted down. Suddenly, a surge of speed pushed the passengers back in their seats as the ship approached the space hole. Rogers tried to concentrate on the shining gold shape in the darkness that was opening in front of them, but space and time were moving too quickly. His eyes were forced closed, his breath trapped in his chest. And then, they were through, and the ship rested in space like a seabird after a storm. They could breathe again.

Below them was the planet they had traveled across the universe to find. Thanos's garden.

"No ships, no armies, no soldiers ... it's just him," Captain Marvel reported back after a quick flight down to the surface of the planet.

Nebula stared out into space. She knew her father. "And that's enough," she whispered.

Thanos had built his life on terror. His world had been filled with darkness, hate, and destruction; one long battle to achieve a single aim—using the six Infinity Stones to destroy half the living creatures in the universe. The Titan had only ever known the smell of fear and death. Until now. The Garden offered him peace.

Here, green hills and forests took the place of the rock and metal walls of his previous homes. The noise of rivers and birds drowned the screams

and gunfire of his memory. The war-maker had become a farmer.

Enormous feet crushed the grass as Thanos moved slowly, unsteadily, through a field. He reached out to pick and examine a fruit, and then turned back and climbed up wooden steps to an old hut. One foot dragged slightly, coming down on each step with a heavy *thud*.

Inside the hut, everything was simple—a table and chair, and a fire for cooking. The firelight showed the face of a man who was at peace with himself.

Then, an old, deep sense of danger made him look up.

A second later, a blinding white light blasted through the side of the hut, throwing Thanos on his back, and a ball of electricity shot through the hole. From it, Captain Marvel leaped onto Thanos like a tiger, pulling back his neck while Bruce Banner and War Machine in their metal fighting suits kept the struggling Titan down. They stretched out the arm that wore the Infinity Gauntlet over the fire.

Through the smoke, Thanos recognized the figures of two more old enemies, Captain America and Black Widow, and then he saw the dark, hate-filled eyes of another familiar face, the Asgardian god Thor. There was a flash of silver metal as the god's ax came down on his arm. The Infinity Gauntlet rolled across the floor, with the hand still inside it, and Thanos roared with pain.

Rocket quickly turned the gauntlet over. The gold metal shone dully in the firelight. But his heart sank. The Infinity Stones were not there. The gauntlet was empty.

"Where are they?" Captain America's voice was dangerously quiet, his anger building.

Captain Marvel leaped onto Thanos like a tiger ...

"The universe needed correction." Thanos looked up at the Avenger. "After that, the Stones had no purpose."

Black Widow was beginning to understand. "So where *are* the Stones?" If she was right, this really was the end. The lost ones, those who had disappeared, would be lost forever.

Thanos's empty eyes stared up at her, and his words killed any hope. "They are gone, reduced to atoms," he said.

"Impossible!" Banner cried. "You used them two days ago!"

"Yes, I used the Stones." Thanos was strangely calm. "I used the Stones to destroy the Stones. It nearly killed me." He remembered the enormous power that had surged through his body, leaving his left side almost useless and his face burned. The pain had been almost unbearable, but it had been necessary. Now, no one would ever be able to change what he had achieved. "The work is done. It always will be. I am ... inevitable."

"He has to be lying." War Machine was desperate.

"My father is many things." Nebula had entered the hut quietly behind the rest. "But he never lies."

Thor's anger was rising and filling his head with a red mist. His failure, his hatred, his pain all combined to push his control over the edge. With a roar, he swung his ax, and this time it was Thanos's head that rolled across the floor.

The small group froze in shocked silence. Thor looked unbelievingly at his hands.

"What did you do?" Rocket spoke for them all.

"I attacked the head ..." Thor said, and walked out of the hut.

"I attacked the head ..." Thor said, and walked out of the hut.

# A Way Forward

**5 years later**

Trees and grass were spreading into the streets and parking lots of New York. A thick silence hung over empty baseball fields, now that the screaming crowds that used to fill them were just ghosts; rivers were clear and becoming home for new forms of wildlife. It seemed that the "disappeared" had been forgotten by nature.

But not by the people who remained.

"We have to take brave, baby steps." Rogers spoke softly to a man who was trying to rebuild his life. "To make ourselves whole again." A tear slid slowly down one of the silent faces in front of him as the small group remembered what they had lost, and looked for a way of living in this new world that was full of holes.

Rogers's own heart was still hurting from loss, but he tried to help others in these meetings. "The world is in our hands," he said. "We have to do something with our lives, or ... why are we still here?" But in his own head, he still questioned: *Why have I survived? What does the future hold?*

In a building in San Francisco where old vans and cars had been stored for the last five years, something moved. It was a rat. This place was never visited by people. Rats and mice were the only living things in the dirt and the dust and the faded painted metal. The old vehicles, waiting for owners that would never come, provided shelter for the increasing number of small creatures and insects in the city.

The rat had found a way into an old, brown van and moved lightly over the wheel and across the controls, looking for something to eat. For a moment, it looked curiously at a button that had suddenly lit up. Not food, it decided.

The next moment, it was running for its life.

Orange and red lights started flashing, and noise filled the van. At first, it was just a low rumble, but then it grew until it sounded like a helicopter fighting to lift off through the roof. The noise source was a ring of bright, gold energy that had opened like a mouth and was spinning so fast that it threatened to shake the old van to pieces.

Suddenly, something tiny shot out of the mouth and crashed through the back door of the van. The lights faded, the noise died, the mouth disappeared. The van was a van again, sitting on the cold floor, empty and lifeless.

"*Ouch!*" Ant-Man—Scott Lang—now full size, sat up uncomfortably, and pushed off some old, smelly cushions. He looked around for Hope van Dyne, his girlfriend, who had been controlling the Quantum Tunnel while he had been in it … and immediately realized that something was wrong. He had entered the tunnel in bright sunshine. There had been people, voices, laughter, and warmth. Now, he was somewhere else, somewhere with a complete absence of light, noise, or heat. And he was surrounded by garbage. What crazy tricks was his mind playing on him?

He waited and tried to slow his breathing.

No, no trick. This was real. Coldness touched the back of his neck.

"Hope!" he called. But the fear in his voice came back to him from the cement walls.

The icy feeling spread further as Lang left the building and walked along the road. Familiar buildings had become unfamiliar. He stared open-

Lang found himself at the edge of a park that had not been left to grow wild.

mouthed at houses, half covered by trees, and piles of garbage spilling over the sidewalk. And there was still that strange silence, which covered everything; the air was thick with it. His city was like a ghost town. No traffic, no people. Hours in the Quantum Realm were years on Earth, and he had returned to a completely different world.

Then, finally, there were people. Lang found himself at the edge of a park that had not been left to grow wild. The grass was short, the paths clean, but the strange silence still hung like a curtain. The people there were not sitting and chatting; they were reading the words on tall standing stones. And there were not just one or two stones—lines of them stretched around the park as far as Lang could see.

On the stones were names. The "disappeared."

Lang tried to swallow his fear. *Cassie*, he thought. *No, please, no, Cassie's name must not be there.* He ran from stone to stone, looking for his daughter's name, hardly daring to breathe. No, no Cassie. But then, he saw a name that completely took his breath away.

Scott Lang.

The familiar shadow on the glass made Cassie's heart jump. *No*, she thought, *it can't be.*

The man on the step was shorter than she remembered. But that was probably because she was taller than she had been five years ago. She ached to reach out to touch him, but she dared not.

It was Lang who put his arms around his daughter and held her face in his hands. Tears came quickly.

"You're so big," he smiled.

Natasha's favorite peanut butter sandwich lay beside her on the desk, dry and curling. She had no interest in it. She had little interest in anything these days. Holographic meetings about various problems around the world were routine and with little point. What could she do? What could any of them do? There was nothing to fight for. The worst had happened. No one could change it.

"We checked the warship that Carol told us about," Rocket's hologram explained. "It was a garbage transport. Thanks, Carol. Now we smell like garbage."

"O.K." Natasha ended the meeting. "This channel is always open to report any problems. Thanks." She sat back, suddenly very tired. She looked again at the sandwich, and away again. Rhodey's hologram was still open. "Where are you?" she asked.

"Mexico." He spoke quietly. "They've found a roomful of bodies. Probably top gangsters. No time to even pull out their guns."

"Another gang?"

Rhodey paused. They both knew what he was going to say. "It was

definitely Barton." Natasha felt a tightness in her chest. Clint Barton was one of her best and oldest friends. His reaction to the disappearance of his family had been to risk his own life, day after day, killing bad guys.

"The bodies, the things he's been doing for the past few years ..." Rhodey imagined the pain that was causing their friend to run wild. "There's a part of me that doesn't even want to find him."

Natasha gave herself a moment before she dared speak. Tears shone in her eyes, but she didn't let them fall. "Will you find out where he's going next?" she asked. "Please."

Rhodey's hologram faded, and then Natasha allowed herself to cry. Hopelessness washed over her.

"I'd offer to cook dinner, but you look pretty upset already." Steve Rogers had come in quietly. He saw, but did not comment on, the mess on Natasha's desk, the dry sandwich, her loose, untidy hair. He took a breath. "I keep telling people to move on ... to grow. Some do. Not us."

Natasha felt the tears threaten again. "I used to have nothing," she said quietly. "Then, I got this—this job, this ... family. And I was better because of it." She paused. "They're gone, but I'm still trying to be better."

Rogers understood exactly what she was saying. The Avengers family joined all of them. Some members were now ghosts, but the family remained. They had to get stronger, not weaker. "I think we both need to get a life," he said softly.

"You first." Natasha gave a small smile.

The camera at the entrance to the building flashed a picture on the screen beside them.

"Hi! Anyone home?" a familiar face called up. "Remember me? Scott

"The bodies, the things he's been doing for the past few years ..." Rhodey imagined the pain that was causing their friend to run wild.

Lang, Ant-Man?" The figure moved closer to the camera. "We met at the airport. I grew really big ..."

*What?* Natasha and Rogers leaned forward to look at the screen.

"Is this an old message?" Rogers asked.

"It's the front gate," Natasha said.

Lang walked up and down the room impatiently. He was talking to himself as well as to the others. He needed to make sense of the ideas that were rushing around, inside his head.

"Have you guys ever studied quantum physics?" Hardly waiting for an answer, he continued. "Well, there's a Quantum Realm, a universe that you can only get into if you're really tiny. Five years ago, I was there, in it. And Hope—she's my ... ." He swallowed. "Well, Hope was controlling the tunnel, and she was going to bring me out, but then, Thanos happened. And I couldn't leave."

Needing to get his ideas out, Lang continued quickly. "But five years *here* is only five hours *there*. Time in the Quantum Realm is different. Is that anybody's sandwich? I'm really hungry." He bit into the sandwich and continued talking excitedly with his mouth full of bread and peanut butter. "So, maybe we could find a way to control the time in the Quantum Realm? We could enter at one point in time and leave it at another point. Like ... like before Thanos?"

The sandwich was disappearing fast. Lang looked at the two Avengers. Could they see the possibilities that he saw?

"Are you talking about a time machine?" Rogers asked slowly.

"No, no, not a time machine. It's more like a ..." Lang started walking again. Then, he stopped. "O.K. Yeah. A time machine," he said. "It's crazy, I know. But I can't stop thinking about it ..."

"Nothing sounds crazy these days." Natasha shook her head.

"Then, who do we talk to about all this?" Lang asked.

# A Difficult Decision

"Lunch time!" Tony Stark sat on the grass in front of a small tent beside the lake near his house. He loved the peacefulness of this spot: the sun on the water, the smell of fall in the air. But more than anything, he loved the little girl whose head came through the entrance of the tent—his and Pepper's daughter, Morgan.

With a shock, he realized that she was wearing an Iron Man-style helmet he had designed as a gift for his wife. His past life as an Avenger had involved a violence that he hoped his daughter would never see or experience.

He picked Morgan up and carried her back to the house. He knew he could not change his daughter. She was curious, like him, always looking for adventure, like him, and pushing the limits, like him. He smiled.

Then, his smile froze. There was a car in front of the house. Some of the people that he felt closest to in the world were waiting. They were the people he least wanted to see right now—Natasha, Rogers, and Lang. The great, brave Tony Stark suddenly felt afraid. Was this perfect life that he had created with Pepper and Morgan going to be threatened?

Stark listened politely to Lang's ideas and then quietly explained why the logic behind his time travel theory wouldn't work; all his knowledge and experience were telling him that this was a completely impossible idea.

"If you do this, you won't come home," he said.

"*I* did," Lang argued.

"No," Stark said. "You accidentally survived. And now you want to commit ... some sort of time heist?" He laughed. "Oh, why didn't we think of that before? Why? Because it's crazy!"

"We could go back, get the Stones, and snap our own fingers." Natasha refused to give up. "We can bring everybody back."

"Or complete what Thanos started and make everything worse." Stark was losing patience. "There is no logical way to do this safely."

"No!" Lang interrupted. "We follow the rules of time travel—we don't talk to ourselves in the past, we don't change things, we ..."

"Are you seriously telling me that your plans to save the universe are based on movies and T.V. shows?" This guy was a joke.

"Tony, we have to try!" Natasha was desperate.

"We *did* try," Stark's eyes went stone cold. "And we failed."

Lang leaned forward. "I know you have a lot to lose. But I lost someone important to me. Lots of people did. And now we have a chance to bring her back—to bring *everyone* back—and you won't even ..." He shook his head, unbelieving.

"That's right, Lang. I won't." Stark tried to speak calmly. The chance of risking Morgan and Pepper was impossible for him to consider. He couldn't allow this idea even the tiniest space in his mind. He walked away.

"He's scared." Rogers understood. Stark had finally found happiness and peace in his life. How could he risk that?

"So, what ...?" Lang's face was white. "Are we just ... going to stop?"

Rogers slowly shook his head. "No," he said. "But I want to do it right. We're going to need a really big brain."

Lang looked back at the house. Tony Stark had the best brain in the world. "Bigger than his?"

The table was full of food. Hulk sat at one end, and Natasha, Rogers, and Lang watched him piling eggs, hamburgers, and toast high on his plate. He needed it. He was enormous.

"I'm confused." Lang spoke for all of them. Was this person Banner, the scientist, or Hulk, the enormous, green-skinned Avenger that Banner became when he was angry? This person looked like Hulk but spoke and behaved calmly, like Banner.

Hulk laughed, a loud, deep Hulk laugh. "I know," he said through a mouthful of eggs. "It's crazy, isn't it? Five years ago, we were beaten by Thanos. But I was beaten *twice*—first as Hulk, then as Banner. So, I decided something. I've always treated Hulk like he was some kind of a disease, but then I thought—maybe he was the cure? I spent eighteen months in a gamma laboratory, and I put the strength and the brain together. Now look at me!" He opened his arms. "I've got the best of both worlds!"

"So," Rogers asked, "what do you think about this time travel idea?"

Hulk shook his head, unsure. "It's a bit outside my scientific area."

Natasha smiled. "Well, so was this." She pointed at his Hulk-Banner body.

**The table was full of food. Hulk sat at one end, and Natasha, Rogers, and Lang watched him piling eggs, hamburgers, and toast high on his plate.**

Drying the plates after dinner, Stark tried not to think about his friends' visit. Then, his eyes settled on a photograph in the kitchen. A young, bright-eyed Peter Parker smiled up at him. And it hurt. Stark had brought Peter into the Avengers family, and Peter had fought with them all to try to destroy Thanos. When the Blip happened—when Thanos used the Infinity Stones to destroy half of all living things—Peter was one of the millions who disappeared. Could Lang be right? Was there a possibility that time travel could bring everyone, including Peter, back? Did Stark have the right to refuse to try?

Something flashed in Tony Stark's big brain. *What if ...?*

Later, in his library, Stark stood back from his desk and stretched, exhausted. He had been trying out a variety of ideas with his AI assistant, FRIDAY, for hours. The screen shone silver-blue and a faint hologram hung in the air above it, continually moving and changing shape. It was getting late, but maybe just one more idea before he stopped for the night ...

He gave FRIDAY instructions for one final possibility, and a new hologram formed. That was fast. Stark was surprised, and moved the hologram around with a finger.

"Don't worry if it doesn't work," he told FRIDAY "I'm just thinking ..."

The next moment, two words knocked Stark back into his chair with shock. The impossible had happened.

MODEL SUCCESSFUL

He had done it.

Stark struggled to realize the importance of the discovery. He had found a way to control time in the Quantum Realm; time travel *was* possible. The question now was—what should he do with the knowledge? If they went back into the past, they risked changing the present. He might return to a world without Morgan.

"Why aren't you in bed, Daddy?" Morgan was sitting on the bottom stair, watching him. As always, Stark felt a surge of love when looking at his daughter.

"Go to sleep, or I'll sell all your toys," he threatened.

Morgan laughed as her father put her back to bed. "Love you three thousand!" she told him.

Stark went to talk to Pepper, to try to make the most difficult decision of his life.

Pepper was reading, and smiled when he sat down.

"Interesting?" Stark asked, and before she could answer, he added quickly, "I solved it."

"We're talking about …?"

"Time travel," Stark said simply. But behind the calm words, Pepper knew that Stark's mind was racing, balancing the present with the past, what he had now with what he and the world had lost.

"That's terrifying." She touched his arm softly.

"Yeah." Stark looked away, almost angrily. Why should he have to choose? "Perhaps I should put the solution in a locked box and sink it in the lake," he said, only half joking.

"But would you be able to rest?" Pepper asked him gently. They both knew the answer.

The small, brown van stood surrounded by scientific equipment in an enormous room in the Avengers building.

"Time Travel Test number one!" Hulk shouted from behind some big, black boxes with switches and wires all over them. "Lang, start the … er … van thing."

Lang opened the van's back doors, and immediately the Quantum Tunnel came alive. Electronic waves pulsed—silver, blue, and gold—from its center. He stood in front of the mouth of the tunnel and closed his helmet.

"I'll send you back a week, you walk around for an hour, and then I'll bring you back. Ten seconds for us." Hulk's thick fingers played over the controls. "Ready?"

Was he? Ready? Lang pictured Hope, and he knew he was. "Yeah."

Hulk flicked a switch, and Lang disappeared. The Avengers held their breath. The tunnel roared as Hulk counted.

"Three–two–one." Hulk flicked another switch, and a body shot out of the tunnel. It was wearing Lang's suit, but the suit was much too big, and the face that looked out through the helmet was a teenager's face.

"This doesn't feel right," a young voice said anxiously.

"Scott?" Natasha asked.

"Yes," the boy said crossly, "I'm Scott!" Hulk's fingers flew over the controls again, and boy-Scott disappeared again into the tunnel. A second later, another body was thrown out. This time a ninety-year-old man narrowed his old eyes to look at them.

Hulk pushed switch after switch. Old-Scott was gone, and another Scott stood in front of them. This time they had to look down. A baby's curious eyes stared up at them.

"He'll grow," Hulk suggested.

"Bring Scott back!" Rogers was losing patience.

"O.K." Hulk banged screens and shook boxes, pulled and pushed different wires. He flicked every switch on the controls. "Turn off the power!" he cried. There was an enormous flash from the tunnel. The body that shot out this time stood up shakily. It was the Lang they knew.

Lang looked uncomfortable. "I've got wet pants," he complained. "I'm not sure if it was old-me, or baby-me ... " He thought for a moment, clearly confused. "Or ... even ... me-me?"

*What a complete disaster*, Rogers thought as he stood outside the building. He needed some fresh air to think, or rethink.

The smell of burning rubber made him turn. A low, black sports car stopped suddenly beside him, and the window rolled down. Tony Stark looked at him over his sunglasses.

"Why so unhappy? Let me guess—he turned into a baby?"

"Among other things."

Stark got out of the car. "That's because you weren't pushing Scott through time, you were pushing time through him. I warned you."

"You did," Rogers agreed. Why was Stark here? Had he come to laugh at them?

"Anyway," Stark said coolly, "I fixed it." He raised his hand to show

Rogers a wristband with a small device in the center. "A time-space GPS."

The corners of Rogers's mouth lifted slightly. This was the old Stark, the Stark who could never walk away from a problem that needed solving.

"I just want peace." Stark and Rogers had been friends for longer than they had been enemies, and they had to bury their differences and work together. Stark took something from the car. "I thought I should give this back to you. I don't want Morgan playing with it."

He handed Captain America's shield to Rogers.

"Thank you, Tony." Rogers was not only talking about the shield.

"But don't tell the others. I didn't bring one for the whole team!" Then, Stark looked at his friend. "We *are* getting the whole team together for this?"

"Yeah," Rogers said. "We're doing that right now."

"We *are* getting the whole team together for this?"

# The Team Back in Action

For some reason, Scott Lang was always hungry. Sitting in the sunshine outside the Avengers building, he was having a well-deserved break, and his stomach rumbled as he lifted his sandwich. The next moment, pieces of lettuce were all over his cheeks, and ketchup slid down his nose. The powerful wind from a landing spaceship had covered him with the contents of the sandwich.

Lang stared at the spaceship, and at the strange characters coming toward him. Spaceships and creatures from other planets were new to him. He was too stunned even to wipe his face.

"Hey, human!" Rocket called. "Where's Big Green?"

Lang tried smiling at Nebula, but she walked straight past him. "Be careful on re-entry," she warned Rhodey through her communication device. "There's a peculiar guy in the landing area."

Hulk passed Nebula and Rhodey as he came out of the Avengers building and gave Lang another sandwich. Then, he walked off to the spaceship with a bag over his shoulder. *Where is he going?* Lang wondered.

Hulk knew that he had a difficult meeting ahead of him. He and Rocket walked through the small fishing village in Norway that had been renamed New Asgard, now home to the small number of Thor's people who remained after most of the population had been destroyed.

"Valkyrie!" Hulk saw a familiar face. The brave Asgardian fighter was one of the survivors of Thanos's attack on her planet. "Great to see you, angry girl!"

He opened his arms wide.

Valkyrie was a little unsure about this new Banner-Hulk combination. It was strange to see the big, green man smiling.

"He won't see you," she said. "He only comes out once a month for supplies." She pointed at a pile of empty beer bottles and fast food boxes.

The smell of old beer and unwashed clothes hit them as they opened the door of the old fisherman's house.

"*Phew!*" Rocket tried to hold his breath. "Something died in here."

Then, a familiar voice thundered, "Have you come to fix the wiring?" And Thor, a beer bottle in one hand, nearly fell over a chair in front of them. For a moment, Hulk and Rocket couldn't speak. Their old friend was nearly as broad as Hulk. His stomach hung over his pants, and he was having trouble speaking clearly.

His face split open in a broad smile. "Boys!" he shouted, and he reached his arms around Hulk and then rubbed Rocket's head and ears—which Rocket did not like at all.

Hulk couldn't believe the change in his friend. The same bright eyes smiled at them, the same deep voice rumbled through his beard, but the last five years had left their mark. Thor had used the house as a cave to hide from the world, and had dulled the guilt and loss he had experienced at the hands of Thanos with beer, food, and super hero computer games.

"Are you all right?" Hulk asked.

"I'm fine. Why? Don't I look all right?"

"You look like melted ice cream." Rocket usually said what he thought.

Hulk didn't wait. "We need your help. There might be a chance we could fix things—you know—Thanos."

Thor's eyes suddenly lost any sign of humor. Silence stretched between him and Hulk like a tight bowstring. Then, he put a hand on Hulk's chest.

"Don't …" His voice trembled. Tears of guilt, fear, and anger were close. "Don't say … that … name."

"Please take your hand off me, Thor," Hulk said gently. "I understand that that guy might scare you."

"Why would I be scared?" The laugh didn't reach Thor's eyes. "I'm the one who killed that guy, remember?"

He opened another beer and stared out the window at the Asgardians in the village—a continual reminder of those he had not been able to save, of his complete uselessness.

But Hulk continued. "You're in a bad state—I know, I've been there myself," he said. "And you know who helped me? *You*."

Thor pushed a handful of chips into his mouth. "Whatever you're offering, I don't care. Goodbye. I don't need rescuing."

"I think we can bring them back," Hulk said. The faint light from the window showed the different emotions struggling on the god's face: fear, guilt, but now hope. Still, he said nothing. "We need you, friend," Hulk said quietly.

Thor's eyes were still shiny with tears, but Hulk could see something else in them, too. Was it a new sense of purpose?

Rocket decided to interrupt this deep, meaningful conversation. "There's beer on the ship," he said loudly.

"What kind?" Thor asked.

"You look like melted ice cream." Rocket usually said what he thought.

The action could be a computer game.

*A dark night on a back street in Tokyo. A killer blasts his way through a night club. Gunfire flashes, knives slice. People run, scream, beg for their lives. The killer follows, leaps from stairs and across hallways. Bodies fall and crash through glass onto the road. Blood wets jackets and patterns sidewalks; the sharp smell mixes with the freshness of falling rain. The killer's final target, dressed in black, hair flat from the rain, stands in front of him on the road, sword raised.*

No, not a computer game. The killer was real. His purpose: to clear the streets around the world of gang members.

"Why are you doing this?" his target screamed. "We never hurt you!"

The killer lifted his own sword. "You lived. Half the planet didn't. *They* got Thanos. *You* got me!"

The man ran at the killer, his sword held like a spear. Not fast enough. The target's fingers went to his throat and came away red.

"What do you want?"

"You can't give me what I want," the killer whispered.

Standing over this last body, the killer wiped his sword clean on his sleeve and lifted his face to the rain. "You shouldn't be here," he said to the person standing behind him on the dark street.

"Neither should you," Natasha said.

**The killer lifted his own sword. "You lived. Half the planet didn't. *They* got Thanos. *You* got me!"**

Barton looked down at the road running with blood and rain. "I have a job to do."

"Is that what this is? All this death—it won't bring your family back." Natasha understood Barton's pain well. "We've found something. A chance maybe?" she said quietly.

Barton turned, his eyes wide, but he shook his head. "No," he said. "No, don't give me hope."

"I'm sorry I couldn't give it to you sooner." Natasha reached out to take her friend's hand.

"Be careful with those!" Lang worried that Hulk's big fingers might crush the small, red tubes containing Pym Particles—their ticket to time travel. The Pym Particles, discovered by the famous scientist Hank Pym, could make people and objects tiny enough to enter the Quantum Realm and regrow afterward, but they only had enough for one return journey to the past each, and one test.

"I'll do it," Barton said and approached the new time machine, built and designed by Stark and Rocket.

"But why can't we just go back in time and kill baby Thanos?" Rhodey asked.

"Because it doesn't work like that. If you change the past, it won't change the future!" Hulk tried to explain. "If you go back into the past, that past becomes your future, and your present—here and now—becomes your past. That can't be changed by your new future."

Confusing.

Barton was going to find out. He was going to test whether it was possible to bring back an object from the past. His destination was his own home before the Blip, and his whole body was tense; he was fearful and anxious about seeing again what he had lost.

An enormous, silver, metal platform had been built over the entrance to the Quantum Tunnel, and Barton, in his Time Suit, stood in the center of the silver circle.

"O.K., Clint, we're going in ... three–two–one." Barton's face shield and helmet closed automatically, and Hulk flicked a switch.

The noise of the tunnel started, and the platform dropped away. Below, spinning rings of gold and red swallowed Barton immediately. It felt like he was being dragged down through the rushing waters of an enormous waterfall. In this new world, he was tinier than an atom and fell uncontrollably through twisting and spinning tunnels of blue clouds. Finally, he was thrown out and landed on something hard that knocked the air out of him.

Barton stands up shakily and looks around. He is in a wooden building, and beside him is the enormous wheel of a farm vehicle. He touches it, unbelieving, and then his eyes are pulled toward the light from an open door. There is a view of a farmhouse. *His* farmhouse.

Barton walks into the sunshine, and immediately he is back on that final day, standing behind Lila as she raises her bow. He can almost feel the warmth of her skin under his hand as he guides her fingers. The memories are so strong that he can hardly breathe. But the yard is empty—apart from a baseball glove that lies at his feet. Gently he picks it up and smiles, his heart full of love for his family.

"Cooper? Where are my headphones?" Is that his daughter, calling to her brother?

"Lila?" Barton whispers. The time alarm on his wristband sounds, but he runs to the farmhouse, steps inside, ... and disappears.

Barton hit the platform hard, and his head was spinning as he struggled to breathe. Natasha helped him stand. He held out the baseball glove. "It worked," he said with a small smile.

Rogers could feel the electricity running through the group, now that they knew there was a real chance for them to get back the Stones.

"O.K.," he said. "So, the 'how' works. Now, we have to think about when and where."

The plan was to go into the past, bring back the Stones, and use them to return the people who had disappeared after Thanos snapped his fingers.

Behind Rogers were six screens, and each showed an Infinity Stone. "We only have enough Pym Particles for one return trip to the past each," he reminded the others. "These Stones have been in a lot of places in history, so we have to pick our time targets carefully."

They needed to choose a time when one or more of their group had been in contact with an Infinity Stone in their own past. And they expected trouble, so each needed support, which meant teams of two. The calculations were tricky.

"First, the Aether. Thor?"

Eyes went to a hologram of the red Reality Stone, and then to Thor, whose dark glasses hid eyes that were probably closed. An empty beer can was balanced on the arm of his chair. Slowly, he stood up, took off his glasses, and rubbed his eyes. His head was feeling a little foggy.

"Er ... to start with, ... er ... it's not really a stone, really." He cleared his throat. "It's more of an angry, muddy sort of thing ..."

He continued with a long and confusing story about his grandfather hiding the Aether, and then the Aether becoming active inside his girlfriend Jane Foster. There was a lot of hesitation and repetition, a lot of twists and turns, and a few tears when he talked about his dead mother.

"But, nothing lasts forever." He smiled wisely, then ended with what he considered to be deep, philosophical words: "The only permanent thing in life is that things are not permanent."

The God of Thunder sat down again, pleased with himself, and went back to sleep.

The group learned from Rocket that the Power Stone was stolen by Peter Quill from the planet Morag, and from Nebula that Thanos had killed her sister, Gamora, when he took the Soul Stone from the planet Vormir.

*O.K.*, Rogers thought. *Teams of two for those three Stones.* But the numbers didn't work for the remaining three—there were not enough

Avengers, not enough Pym Particles. But then, Natasha made an important connection.

From lying on her back in the middle of papers and food wrappers, exhausted by the lengthy discussions, she suddenly sat up.

"Guys!" she cried. "If we choose the right year, there are three Stones in New York—at the same time."

She was right. In the year 2012, the Time Stone, the Space Stone, and the Mind Stone were all in New York.

*Yes,* Rogers thought. *Of course!* One team could get all three Stones from New York in one journey. Another team could go to Asgard to get the Reality Stone. And a third team could travel to Morag for the Power Stone, and continue to Vormir for the Soul Stone. It was a plan. There were many things that could go wrong, but it was a plan.

The group learned from Rocket that the Power Stone was stolen by Peter Quill from the planet Morag, and from Nebula that Thanos had exchanged the life of his daughter, Gamora, for the Soul Stone on the planet Vormir.

# Into Another Time

"Six Stones, three teams, one chance," Rogers told the Avengers, as they stood, waiting, on the Quantum Platform. "Five years ago, we lost." He looked around the circle. "All of us. We lost friends, we lost family, and we lost part of ourselves. Today we have a chance to take it all back."

He paused, thinking about the importance of this moment, about the opportunity they had to give life back to millions of people. He needed to balance his words carefully, giving the teams confidence but also warning them about the results of failure. They would never have this chance again.

"You know what to do—get the Stones, bring them back here."

The Avengers joined hands.

"One round trip each," Rogers continued calmly. "No mistakes. Most of us are going to places we know, but that doesn't mean we know what to expect. Be careful. Support each other. This is the fight of our lives, and we're going to win—whatever we have to do." Rogers looked directly at Stark, who lifted his head slightly in recognition of their friendship and understanding. Once again, they were fighting on the same side. "Good luck."

There was a tense silence.

Then, Rocket broke it. "Good speech!"

"You heard the man, hit those keys!" Stark called. Switches were flicked, and Hulk joined the circle.

Each Avenger touched his or her wristband, and helmets closed. Each had a different picture in his or her mind. Barton saw his family, Nebula saw her sister, Stark saw Peter Parker ... Each picture represented what the world had lost. They all knew that Rogers was right. This was going to be the fight of their lives.

"See you in a minute," Natasha said to Rogers. The tunnel became active with a roaring noise, like the sound of a jet plane, and a spinning light show of flashing red and gold. The platform fell away, and the Avengers disappeared into the pulsing mouth below. Each team was racing through different twisted tunnels at speeds much greater than anything they could ever have imagined.

### New York, 2012

Captain America, Hulk, Ant-Man, and Iron Man surface on a New York street, where the air is thick with battle smoke and the noise of gunfire and breaking glass. The Chitauri, enemies from space that are helping Thor's brother Loki gain control of Earth, are attacking from the air and the ground in great numbers. Buildings and streets are covered with the screaming, insect-like creatures.

"All right," Captain America tells the team. "We all know what we're doing. There are two Stones uptown, one down. Stay low, and watch the clock ..."

He is interrupted by a familiar roar. At the end of the street, a car crashes down on a Chitauri creature, and the enormous, green body of Hulk 2012 angrily jumps up and down on it. The Avengers 2012 are fighting back.

Rogers looks at Hulk 2023, who drops his head in embarrassment. "Maybe you should throw a few things around while you're on your way?" he suggests.

"O.K." Unenthusiastically, Hulk walks forward with his great, green arms lifted. "*Ahhh!*"

He practices a roar, but it sounds more like a sick dog than a lion. He hits a car roof with his hand, and throws a motorcycle across the road. He makes his way uptown to find and take the Time Stone from the home of the sorcerer, Doctor Strange.

**The Avengers 2012 are fighting back.**

Outside the building, Hulk '23 sees the Chitauri weapons in the air, but he does not see the woman who is standing silently, alone on the roof. He cannot see the strange movements she is making with her arms, which direct fireballs at the attacking ships. Her hands seem to be circled by gold rings of energy, and wherever she points a Chitauri ship crashes and bursts into flames.

Hulk leaps on to the roof and moves toward a doorway, but a sharp voice stops him.

"Don't go in there," the Ancient One says. "We've just washed the floors." The woman is tall and dressed in gold.

Unsure exactly how to explain his presence, Hulk tells her, "I'm looking for Doctor Strange." It is the truth—but not all of it.

The woman's eyes narrow slightly. "I'm afraid you're five years too early," she says. "At this moment, Stephen Strange is operating on a patient at a hospital about twenty blocks away."

Hulk is confused. How can this woman know the future? Then, he sees what she is wearing around her neck, and he understands: it is the Eye of Agamotto, containing the Time Stone. His target.

"What do you want from Doctor Strange?" the woman asks.

Hulk smiles and points a thick, green finger at the Stone. "That, actually."

She smiles back politely. "I'm afraid not."

"Sorry, I wasn't asking—I need that Stone." Hulk covers the space between them quickly, his hand reaching out for the Stone.

"You don't want to do that," she says, and places her hand on his chest. Lightning flashes from her fingers, Hulk is thrown backward, and then something amazing happens: he splits in two. The physical Hulk body lies on the stone floor, while the spirit of Banner is left floating in front of the Ancient One, looking down at his checked shirt and wondering—what?—how?

The most powerful sorcerer of them all smiles. "Now, let's start again, shall we?" she suggests calmly.

### Asgard, 2013

Thor is starting to think that coming back to his father's palace on Asgard was not a good idea; there are too many bad memories here. Jane is one of them. He sees her as he and Rocket hide in one of the great halls, watching. A long time ago, that lovely woman was his girlfriend. Oh, if he could go back ... Wait, he *is* back, but he can't ...

"O.K., big man," Rocket tells him. "Here's the plan. You go and charm her, and while you do that, I pull the Reality Stone out from inside her, and we're done."

Thor's mouth feels suddenly very dry, and any confidence he had on the Quantum Platform is rapidly disappearing. A solution presents itself immediately.

"I'll be right back." He starts to walk away. "My, er ... father's wine store

Lightning flashes from her fingers, Hulk is thrown backward, and then something amazing happens: he splits in two.

is just down here. He used to have a wonderful supply of Aakonian beer ..."

But before he can move, footsteps sound on the stone floor, and he and Rocket press themselves against the wall again.

A beautiful woman is talking to some ladies. "Who's the pretty one?" Rocket asks.

Thor swallows. "It's my mother," he whispers. "She dies today." Tears threaten; he hasn't seen her for so long. "I shouldn't be here," he says and turns away. "This is wrong, it's a bad idea. I can't do this. I can't ..."

His voice rises, uncontrolled, until he feels the sting of Rocket's hand on his cheek. His mouth falls open. This small creature has dared to hit the God of Thunder. It is even more shocking than seeing his mother, who has been dead for more than ten years.

"Listen." Rocket forces the big man to look at him. "You think you're the only one who lost people? I lost the only family I ever had—Quill, Groot, Drax, all gone. Yeah, you miss your mom, but she's gone—I mean, *really* gone. There are plenty of people who are only *kind of* gone and you can help them." This is new for Rocket. He usually hides his feelings with jokes. But Thor needs to be shaken out of his self-pity and guilt. "So, is it too much to ask you to brush all the bits of bread out of your beard and talk nicely to the lady, while I get the Stone?"

Thor takes a deep breath. "O.K.," he says, then almost immediately, "No, I can't do this!"

Rocket tries to remain patient, not something he is good at. "Stop this! You can do it!" It is like talking to a child with first-day-at-school nerves. "All right?"

"Yes," Thor finally agrees, and Rocket turns again to watch Jane.

Behind him, Thor concentrates. "I can do this. I can do this. I can do

this," he repeats. Then, "No, I can't do this."

When Rocket turns back, Thor has gone.

### Morag, 2014

Morag is an unfriendly planet. Electrical storms keep visitors away, and little survives there apart from some nasty little creatures with sharp teeth. Black Widow kicks one as it tries to bite her foot. Above her, a two-man spaceship comes down to the planet's surface from below the Guardians of the Galaxy's larger ship.

The plan is working. Nebula and War Machine will stay on Morag to find the Power Stone, while Black Widow and Hawkeye continue in the Guardians' spaceship to the planet Vormir. Their target—the Soul Stone.

"Take care, O.K.?" Black Widow says. Will they ever see each other again? It feels like a complicated game of chance, and she desperately hopes that luck is on their side. Looking forward, not back, she and Hawkeye take the pilots' seats at the front of the spaceship.

The speed of the ship pulls them breathlessly through space toward a bright, golden jump point, and as the stars fly past in streams of shining blue, the speed of the ride makes their hearts race. In spite of the danger ahead, the two friends share a secret smile. If it is their last adventure together, it is going to be an exciting one.

When the ship disappears into space, War Machine feels a sudden fear of what is going to happen to them on this cold, lonely planet. It is like a land of ghosts. Dead trees raise branches under a sky heavy with dark clouds. Purple lightning cuts through the atmosphere, and the rumble of thunder never stops. Clouds of black dust drift across the land, sometimes uncovering enormous towers of rock.

"We're not the only ones in 2014 looking for the Stones."

War Machine looks around at the emptiness. He is used to fighting in wars and battles, not in dead, unreal places like this. "So, we just wait for this Quill guy to arrive, and then he leads us to the Power Stone, is that it?" he checks with Nebula.

"Let's hide." She turns and starts to walk toward some rocks. "We're not the only ones in 2014 looking for the Stones."

"What are you talking about? Who else?"

Nebula turns. A rare emotion flashes in her eyes. "My father, my sister." Her voice is very low. She pauses and then looks at War Machine directly. "And me," she says.

"You?" War Machine asks. "Where are you right now?"

Nebula 2014 screams and brings her sword hard down on her enemy—a Korbinite soldier fighting Thanos's army—but he rises again. This time he blasts Nebula up into the smoke-filled air, and she lands on her back close to the ship's energy source, which shoots pure white power upward. One push and ... but something moves in the smoke. He turns as a figure leaps, spins, and kicks him into the streaming white energy. His screams die quickly.

Gamora 2014 offers a hand to her sister.

"I didn't ask for your help," Nebula says angrily. She has a deep hatred of Gamora, who has always been preferred by their father, Thanos. Nebula is never good enough, and he punishes her hard for that.

"Father wants to see us," Gamora says. "He's found an Infinity Stone. On a planet called Morag."

Nebula considers this. "Then his plan has begun."

Moments later, they are standing in front of the enormous figure of their father. His power is unquestionable. In his face and voice are cold ambition and cruelty.

"We have discovered where the Power Stone is." Thanos's words are slow, his voice like an icy breath of wind. "I'm sending *you*."

"We will not fail you," Nebula whispers. But a sudden, blinding pain in

**A hologram appears in front of them.**

her head knocks her to her knees and drags a scream from her mouth. The electrical connections in her brain seem to be on fire, and she shakes her head desperately. Suddenly, her whole body goes stiff, and a blue beam of light comes from her left eye. A hologram appears in front of them.

A metal-suited soldier floats in the blue light. *"So, we just wait for this Quill guy to arrive, and then he leads us to the Power Stone, is that it?"* It is War Machine. His shape moves with the waves of light, but his words are clear.

Then, a familiar voice replies to his. *"Let's hide,"* another Nebula whispers. *"We're not the only ones in 2014 looking for the Stones."*

Then, the hologram dies, bringing another blast of pain. Nebula screams again and hits her own head to try to fight it.

"Who was that?" Gamora kneels beside her sister.

"I ... don't ... know ..." Nebula can hardly speak. A knife seems to be splitting her head in two.

Gamora looks at her father. "Perhaps her electrical connections were damaged in battle." She fears what Thanos might do to Nebula next.

The big Titan senses warning signals. Is there a threat to his master plan to gain all six Infinity Stones? It needs to be explored and removed quickly and completely, whatever the cost. The source of the hologram that showed itself through Nebula's eyes is the key to answering the question. Nothing or no one, most certainly not his daughter, will threaten what he intends for the universe.

He touches his sword to Nebula's chin and forces her head up. "Bring her to my ship," he tells Gamora.

### New York, 2012

Iron Man and Captain America divide the work. Two Stones, two "time heists," two Avengers. Events follow almost faster than the speed of the Quantum Tunnel.

It has been a hard day for Avengers '12, and the physical effort and nervous energy spent battling the Chitauri have exhausted them. But it was worth it. The attack is over, and the creatures have been sent back to their own space and time, Loki is a prisoner, and the Scepter with the Mind Stone and the Tesseract with the Space Stone are in safe hands. Black Widow gives the case with the Scepter to a group of armed guards.

"Who are *they?*" Ant-Man whispers loudly from his viewing point on Iron Man 2023's shoulder, out of sight of the 2012 group.

"HYDRA, an enemy organization," Iron Man tells him. "But we didn't know that then!"

The guards take the elevator down, and Iron Man '23 uses his heat-detector glasses to follow the progress of the stone. "Steve, it's getting close!" he warns Captain America, who is ready to steal the Mind Stone.

As Captain America 2023 boards the elevator on the 14th floor, he gets angry looks from the guards but a whispered "For HYDRA" in the ear of their leader relaxes the tension. Captain America exits the elevator with the case, the Scepter, and a small smile. *Easy!* he thinks. *Job nearly done!*

Iron Man's job is not, and unfortunately it depends on his insect friend. Still on the top floor, the Tesseract is put in another case, watched by the Avengers '12, who are ready to carry it to safety.

"Flick me!" tiny Ant-Man whispers urgently. With a quick movement, he is thrown through the air onto Iron Man 2012's sleeve and immediately hides himself in the collar. His role will come later.

Loki has been defeated, his plans for control of Earth ruined, but he appears to be the only one who is relaxed. The "god of evil tricks" plays another trick, here among his defeaters, by shape-changing into Captain America for a moment, but no one is amused. *Seriously*, he thinks, *what do these guys do for a laugh?*

They crowd into the elevator, leaving no space for the enormous, green Hulk, who is forced to take the stairs all the way down to the ground floor. They can hear his deep, rough voice rumbling loudly: "Take the stairs, I HATE the stairs!" and his heavy footsteps *thump*, as the elevator drops like lightning, floor by floor, until they reach ground level. Officials are waiting for them.

Secretary Pierce, also at the time an unknown enemy, demands that Iron Man '12 give him Loki and control of the Tesseract. This was not the plan. Thor enters the argument; words at first polite, and then angrier, are exchanged, and soon the man from S.H.I.E.L.D. and the Avengers '12 are physically struggling over the case, almost forgetting about Loki. Iron Man '23, in a guard's uniform, whispers instructions to Ant-Man, who is now in Iron Man '12's hair.

"Let's go!" Iron Man '12 rubs his beard absently as Ant-Man drops down his neck, behind his shirt, and—becoming even tinier—enters the power source on his chest. It is unreal to be inside the most amazing energy source, inside the most amazing hero of them all. He sees a long tube, shining blue light, and stretches his tiny arms around it.

The struggle is getting violent. Pierce is trying to take the Tesseract; Iron Man '12 and Thor are fighting equally hard to keep control.

"Disconnect the source," Iron Man '23, watching the fight from a distance, calls urgently. "Now!" Ant-Man pulls as hard as he can, but the connector is tight. Arms burning with the effort, he tries again and this time the connection breaks free.

"*Ahh!*" Iron Man '12 holds his chest, his eyes roll back, and he hits the floor hard, his whole body shaking. Immediately, attention is dragged away from the case. Is Iron Man, the greatest super hero of them all, dying? Iron Man '23 is unconcerned. He knows it is just a small heart attack, to take away their attention. But now his role in their daring game is really beginning. Ant-Man escapes the shaking body and, with strength much greater than his size, kicks the case across the floor to Iron Man '23, who picks it up and walks calmly across to the door. He gives a small smile. Job nearly done!

But they have not considered Hulk '12.

The green guy's simple mind is boiling after thundering down hundreds and hundreds of stairs, and he blasts through the door in full Hulk anger. "No stairs!" he roars.

The door crashes into Iron Man '23, who is thrown onto his back. The case breaks open, the Tesseract flies through the air, and it lands in front of an amused Loki, who calmly picks it up. *Such strange twists in life*, he thinks with amusement, as the Tesseract shines blue in his hands. Then Loki, the clever magician, and the Tesseract are swallowed in a cloud of blue-black smoke.

On his back, Iron Man '23 lies still, angry at himself, angry at everyone. It seemed much too easy. The job is not done, not even nearly. They need *six* Stones, not five. What now?

Captain America's smile does not last long either. On the 14th floor, his shield in one hand and the case with the Scepter in the other, he finds himself on a glass bridge connecting sections of the building, and then he freezes. He is facing a mirror.

Captain America 2012 is standing in front of him.

**But they have not considered Hulk '12.**

# Successes and Failures

**New York, 2012**

Calmly, Captain America '12 speaks into his radio. "I have eyes on Loki, 14th floor." In his mind, the man in front of him is Loki, using his shape-changing tricks again.

Captain America '23 slowly puts down the case and stands. "I am not Loki," he says. "And I do not want to hurt you."

The fight is inevitable. Captain America '12 throws himself at his double, who has no choice and hits back. But both Captain Americas are the same: matching powers, equal strength, the same commitment. How can it end? Shield crashes into shield, body thunders into body.

"I can do this all day," Captain America '12 smiles.

"I know, I know," Captain America '23 admits. "Me, too, friend."

The power of the fighting bodies throws the shields through the glass walls of the bridge, and the case drops down to the floor below, freeing the Scepter. The noise confuses the fighters, and they crash through the hole in the glass, falling, too, through walkway after walkway. Breathless, but not beaten, they lie face down on the ground. Captain America '12 turns to finish "Loki," but he sees something that makes him pause.

A photograph has fallen out of the enemy's pocket. It stuns him. He knows that woman—oh, he knows her so well. It's Peggy Carter, the love of his life. Captain America '23 takes advantage and lifts himself to attack again. The Scepter is in sight, but his younger self is quick to react and gets his arm around his neck, pulling tighter and tighter, cutting off his airway. Captain America '23's head is beginning to go foggy, their plan is failing, but he has one last chance.

"Bucky," he struggles to say. "Bucky is alive."

Captain America '12 stops, shocked—Bucky, his protector, his hero, his friend, long thought dead? His fingers relax slightly.

All Captain America '23 needs is that one, small chance. One arm crashes into the side of Captain America '12's head and the other pushes the Scepter with the Mind Stone into '12's heart. It will stun him for long enough. Captain America '23 stands shakily, picks up the photograph, and holds the Scepter tightly. He looks at his old body for a moment. *Sorry*, he thinks. *That was unfair. But you'd do the same. In fact, yeah, you* have *done the same.*

Uptown, Banner is using his most persuasive scientific reasons to fight the Ancient One's objections, but explanations are hard.

The sorcerer remains calm, her reply considered and logical. "If I give up the Time Stone to help *your* reality, I am risking my own," she says calmly.

Her hand sweeps through the air like a knife, creating a long, pulsing beam of golden light that stretches between her and Banner and beyond the rooftop. "The Infinity Stones create what you experience as the line of time. Remove one of the Stones, and that line splits."

Six colored Stones circle the pulsing arrow of gold. She flicks the green one out of the circle, and the golden beam breaks; a dark line branches off along a close but different path. Banner watches, amazed.

"That may be good for your reality," she continues, "but not *my* new one." Her eyes follow the black line. "In this new branch reality, without our chief weapon against the dark forces, our world will be badly threatened—millions will suffer." Her clear, green eyes look steadily into Banner's. "Tell me, Doctor. Can your science prevent all that?"

"No." Banner pauses, understanding exactly what she means. "But we can repair the split," he says excitedly. "When we've used the Stones, we can return each one to the time it was taken. In that reality, it never left."

He gently pushes the green Stone back into the circle, and the dark line re-joins the golden time-line.

The Ancient One considers his words, balancing different futures in her mind. The brightness in her eyes fades a little. "But to do that, you will need to survive," she says quietly.

"I will." Banner has no more to offer her, no other way to beg. "*We* will. I promise."

"I can't risk this reality on a promise." The woman's mouth is a tight line. "It is my duty as Sorcerer Supreme to protect the Time Stone."

Banner plays his last card. "Then why does Strange give it away?"

The Ancient One looks shocked. "Willingly?"

"Yes—to Thanos."

"Why?"

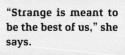

"Strange is meant to be the best of us," she says.

"I don't know why. Perhaps he made a mistake," Banner says, and yes, it was a mistake. The Time Stone as payment for Stark's life had cost the lives of half the universe, and filled Stark with guilt for the rest of his life.

All color leaves the Ancient One's face. She lifts her head and moves closer to Hulk, searching his eyes for lies. She sees none.

"Or perhaps *I* did," she says softly.

Still staring into Banner's eyes, she stretches out a hand. The physical Hulk body lifts from the floor, and Banner's spirit form melts back into it. Once again, Hulk, the Avenger, stands in front of her.

Her hands then drop to her waist, where the Eye of Agamotto rests on its chain. Her fingers move over it and the metal Eye opens, uncovering its bright, shining green secret. The Ancient One holds the Infinity Stone in her hand for a moment and looks up to Hulk.

"Strange is meant to be the best of us," she says.

"Then he did it for a reason." Hulk's breath is caught in the magic of both the Stone and her trust. The weight of so many more lifetimes rests with him and his friends.

"I fear you are right." Her voice trembles, but her hand is firm as she passes the Time Stone to Hulk. She closes his fingers over it tightly and holds his hands for a moment. "I am depending on you," she says. "We all are."

### Space, 2014

Nebula '14 is floating in the dark on *Sanctuary II*, Thanos's ship. She hangs there, face down, unable to move or speak as Thanos connects a mechanical arm to the back of her head.

"Show me her memory files," he orders his assistant, Ebony Maw, who is working the controls.

"Sir, the files are confused. It appears that another consciousness is sharing the same network. Another Nebula." His eyes narrow. "From nine years in the future."

Thanos's brain tries to make sense of what seems impossible. "Where is this other Nebula now?"

Ebony Maw flicks a switch. "On Morag, my lord."

Thanos thinks quickly. "Search the double's memory files for any mention of the Infinity Stones."

Ebony Maw is happy to obey. He enjoys causing pain, and these brain searches certainly cause Nebula to suffer. Gamora '14 watches, unable to interrupt.

Suddenly, the blue electric beam shoots from Nebula's left eye again. This time, more ghostly figures move wave-like in the mist.

*These Stones have been in a lot of places in history," one man, holding a coffee cup, says, "so we have to pick our time targets carefully."*

"Freeze!" Thanos orders. He examines the figures. He knows these people. "Avengers!" His cold voice is full of disgust. Then, he notices a cloudy figure in the background. "Maw—make that clearer!"

Ebony Maw moves the switches. The shape grows, and the details become sharper. A gray and blue head stares at them from the hologram; the eyes are black and hard. It is a familiar face—the face from which the hologram is being shone now. Nebula.

"Two Nebulas!" Gamora is stunned.

"No, the same Nebula from two different times." Now, Thanos understands. The threat that he has sensed is real.

"We go to Morag," he whispers.

The fire continues to comb through both Nebulas' memories, inside his daughter's aching head, but Thanos has no interest in her suffering.

**Asgard, 2013**

Thor's mother, Frigga, senses something unusual in the atmosphere of the Great Hall; she was raised by sorcerers and has unusual powers. She knows her son is close. She can also feel that he is anxious.

"What are you doing?" she whispers from behind his shoulder.

"*Ahh!*" Thor's heart jumps. Then, he sees it is his mother—his wonderful, beautiful mother—and he is both happy and ashamed; he knows she will see the secrets in his eyes.

But he lies. And the God of Thunder is not good at lying. "Er ... I was just ... taking a walk ..." he tries.

Frigga looks at her son's strange clothes, his large stomach, his dirty hair, and the eyes that do not meet hers. She shakes her head slightly. "You're not the Thor I know at all, are you?" she asks gently.

"Yes, I am," he lies again bravely.

Frigga takes his face in her hands. Her touch is so soft that he wants to cry. "The future hasn't been kind to you, has it?"

Now the tears do come, and the powerful God of Thunder is a child again, crying in his mother's arms. The years fade away, and the smell of his mother's hair takes him back to a time of innocence, when no one depended on him, when his future was an exciting, empty sheet to fill with brave actions and pride.

He cries until Frigga's arms and soft voice give him the strength to tell her the whole terrible story; how guilt and shame have left him weak and powerless to make things right again, ever.

"... Thanos's head was over there—and his body was over *there*." Thor looks up; his eyes are red. "I was too late," he says simply. "I was just standing there. A fool with an ax."

Frigga sits beside her son. "No, not a fool," she says and then adds, "but a failure—yes. And that makes you exactly like everyone else."

"I'm not supposed to be like everyone else." The weight of being a hero is heavy, and he truly feels himself sinking under it. "People expect things from me."

Frigga cannot take the weight for her son, but she can help him carry it. "It's what you *succeed* in that is important."

"GET THE RABBIT!" Shouting fills the Great Hall, as the heavy boots of Asgardians run across the stone.

"Thor! I got it!" Rocket cries as he runs, the tube of the red Aether substance—the Reality Stone—held tightly in one hand. Jane did not even notice the small creature in her room.

"Hi!" he says to Frigga. "You must be mom!" He turns to Thor. "Let's go!"

"If we had more time ..." Thor holds Frigga's hands.

"Go and be the man you are meant to be," she smiles, and they hold each other. "I love you. And eat a salad!" When they step apart, Thor's eyes are brighter and his forehead smoother.

"Three–two ..." Rocket counts, impatiently.

"No, wait," Thor cries. He stretches out his left arm, drops his eyes, and concentrates, waiting. *For what?* Rocket wonders.

Thor half-opens one eye and looks through the window. *Am I, can I, will it? Please.* He closes the eye again and suddenly—*whoosh!* A heavy object flies through the window into his hand. Thor looks at the magic hammer in his hand—Mjolnir—his face full of wonder and disbelief. He laughs, a strong, joyful laugh. The old Thor is back.

"I am still worthy!"

Rocket touches his wristband.

### Morag, 2014

Music blasts through Peter Quill's headphones: sounds of the '70s, strong beat, loud. He sings—shouts—with the song, as he dances over rocks, slides through water and dust bowls, twists between bone-white trees, and kicks any small creatures that dare to cross his path. The cold, lonely emptiness of Morag doesn't affect him—the place is just another

"I am still worthy!"

source of income. He is there for a valuable prize, and Quill is a very happy thief. Music and money—what more could he wish for?

"So, he's a fool?" War Machine asks Nebula, watching the pumping arms and the swinging shoulders of this strange character wearing a long, black, leather coat from another century.

"Yes," she admits slowly. The Peter Quill she knew had been kind, generous, caring, and ... yes ... a little crazy, too.

"Da–da–da, da–da–da, de–dah ... *Oof!*" A blow to the side of the head from War Machine stops the singer and the song. The light in Quill's eyes goes out, and he is face down in the white dust, the music playing to deaf ears.

Nebula's quick fingers go through the contents of Quill's bag and find a long, thin, metal tube.

"The tool of a thief," Nebula whispers and is soon running to the black, metal doors of an ancient building. The tool flashes in her hand, and with a quick twist the lock opens. Behind the heavy doors, there is an inky blackness, but at its heart a shower of light drops from the roof. Floating inside is a shining ball of purple metal.

"Wait!" War Machine holds Nebula back. "When you enter a place called 'The Temple of the Power Stone,' there are going to be traps, right?

**It is a strong force field of powerful energy that protects the Stone, but Nebula pushes her metal hand into it.**

Like poisoned arrows and things?"

Nebula ignores him and goes straight to the purple shower. It is a strong force field of powerful energy that protects the Stone, but Nebula pushes her metal hand into it. The field stretches like a skin until, finally, she is through it and holds the metal ball in her hand.

Nebula drops the Power Stone into War Machine's protective glove. She looks at the remains of her metal fingers, burned away by the force field. "I wasn't always like this," she says, remembering Thanos and how he had replaced parts of her body with metal. But then, she experiences a strange satisfaction. The Power Stone is theirs, and she will have her revenge.

"Let's go!" They touch their wristbands. "Three–two–one ..." War Machine counts down ... and he disappears, back to 2023.

Nebula sees his empty space in front of her. Why? They were supposed to return together. It takes hardly a second for her to realize that a greater power than theirs is holding her in this place, for an even more powerful reason. Pain explodes inside her brain, and she falls screaming, holding her head, as the blue hologram shoots from her left eye. Thanos has connected the networks of the two Nebulas.

On Thanos's ship, the beam from Nebula '14's brain continues to show scenes from the future. Now, the faint shape of his own head appears in the waves of blue: older, more tired, and marked on one side with burns.

"*Where are they?*" *a voice outside the hologram demands.*

"*The universe needed correction,*" *Thanos whispers.*

As she stands beside her father, horror rises in Gamora '14's chest. She knows his plan, but she has never believed it possible for him to achieve it.

"*So where are the Stones?*" *a ghostly figure shouts.*

*A laugh, empty of humor, rumbles from Thanos as he looks up at the figures, satisfaction in his dead eyes.* "*They are gone, reduced to atoms. I used the Stones to destroy the Stones. It nearly killed me.*"

*He sinks back, content. Nothing can be changed. The disappeared cannot be brought back.* "The work is done. It always will be. I am ... inevitable."

The figures fade, but Gamora's face is still washed blue in the light from her sister's eye. She risks a question: "What did you do?"

"Nothing," her father says, "yet. They're not trying to stop something I'm going to do in *our* time—they're trying to change something I've already done in *theirs*." Curious, he walks around the picture of his head, frozen in the hologram, examining it.

Finally, Gamora understands. "The Stones," she whispers.

Yes. Thanos almost smiles. He succeeded. The hologram tells him that. He found all the Stones. He used them. He changed the universe.

Ebony Maw restarts the hologram and Nebula 2023's voice is decisive. *"My father is many things. But he never lies."*

*Then, a flash of lightning splits the hologram waves, and Thanos's head is sliced from his body. The enormous Titan roars for the final time.*

Ebony Maw immediately wraps a chain around Nebula '14's neck as she hangs in the air, unable to free herself. It grows tighter. Death is a moment away. And, in these dying seconds, she has no understanding of the reason.

"Sir," Ebony Maw says, unaffected by her increasing pain, "your daughter is an enemy."

"I would never, never hurt you, Father," Nebula whispers. "Never!"

"I know." Thanos breaks the chain, and almost tenderly turns her frightened face to his, his eyes searching deep into hers. "And you will

On Thanos's ship, the beam from Nebula '14's brain continues to show scenes from the future.

have the chance to prove it," he says.

His words carry both a promise and a threat.

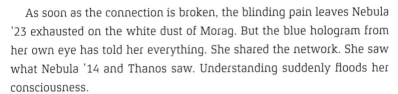

As soon as the connection is broken, the blinding pain leaves Nebula '23 exhausted on the white dust of Morag. But the blue hologram from her own eye has told her everything. She shared the network. She saw what Nebula '14 and Thanos saw. Understanding suddenly floods her consciousness.

"He knows!" she cries. Thanos can defeat them, even from the past.

Desperately, she runs to the Guardians' spaceship and shouts into the communication device. "Barton, Natasha, anyone?" Nebula, who has rarely shown emotion, is now unable to stop herself. She is shaking with a fear greater than she has ever known.

There is no answer. "*Thanos knows!*" she screams again to whoever might hear her. "He ... knows ..." ... and then, her voice fades.

Darkness covers the ship like a thundercloud, and a powerful light beams down. The ship is lifted. Nebula knows what is waiting for her. Thanos knows the part she has played. He knows how she has changed and what she has become. In her soul, she knows how he will make her pay, and how he will kill her spirit; he will force her to destroy the people who have saved her from herself.

**Curious, he walks around the picture of his head, frozen in the hologram, examining it.**

# Strange Meetings

**New York, 2012**

It is impossible. Six Stones, six chances, and Loki has ruined everything; the Tesseract has gone, who knows where. Captain America hears the news from Iron Man, as he re-joins him and Ant-Man on the street.

Iron Man's anger with himself is just under control. Ant-Man is less calm. His words chase around his head and explode from his mouth like bullets: "You said we had one chance at this. Six Stones or nothing. Six chances or nothing, you said," he shouts. "Six chances or *nothing!*"

His feet will not stay still; they beat out his words, backward, forward. He faces Iron Man, accusingly. "You didn't want the time-heist, you *ruined* the time-heist! There is *no* second chance. We're not going anywhere else. We have one Pym Particle left each. If we use that, we're not going home!"

The words are annoying background noise as Iron Man thinks through the situation. *We had six journeys. It is therefore impossible to make another one to regain the Tesseract—or is it?* Iron Man's brain suddenly makes a great leap. The guilt of losing the Tesseract fades, and he sees a possibility, a very faint possibility ... *Yes!*

"I know!" he shouts. "There's another way. We can get the Tesseract back *and* get new Pym Particles so that we can return." He faces Captain

America, his heart jumping a little. Will his old friend risk it? Will he support him this time? "Shall we take a little walk back into the distant past, Steve? To an army base in New Jersey?"

Captain America remembers and understands. It is a brilliant idea. His face remains calm, but calculations are dancing around in his brain.

"When were they there at the same time?" he asks. "Do you know?"

Iron Man gives a strange smile. "I think I do. Trust me?"

Captain America's blue eyes lock with Iron Man's. He has never stopped trusting him. "O.K."

Iron Man sets new numbers on their wristbands.

"Hey!" Ant-Man shouts. "Are we *all* going?"

Captain America throws him the Scepter, with hardly a look. Ant-Man can be helpful, but this is a job for the old team, a very old team. "No. Take this back," he calls.

Ant-Man stares at the empty spaces on the street.

**New Jersey Army Base, 1970**

It is a dangerous return for both Rogers and Stark. The younger Steve Rogers, with his exceptional strength, has not yet been found in the ice, but his face is well-known. For Stark, there is another risk.

Dressed as an officer and a scientist, they join the busy members of the base. Uniforms rush around them, carrying files and cups, running to meetings, exchanging greetings, pushing doors. But one building, with no windows, is experiencing little activity. Few people enter, and those who do go in enter quickly and quietly. The two Avengers share a smile. They have identified their target.

Using his heat-detecting glasses, Stark sees through the walls, and watches people going down in an elevator. The science laboratories are underground. That is where the Tesseract will be hidden, and where Pym works. That is where they need to be.

Inside, Stark is first to exit the elevator: his target, the Tesseract. He finds himself in a long, badly lit, but luckily empty room. Computer screens shine green on tables covered with papers and files, and lining the walls are locked metal containers. These almost certainly store many legally and illegally developed scientific secrets. Stark moves quickly past the tables, chairs, and containers, his heart beginning to race. Time is short. The Tesseract is here, in one of these. He knows it. But which one? The glasses, also designed to detect the signals given off by the Infinity Stones—their signature—read negative time after time, until ... finally. A positive reaction. A quick look over his shoulder, and he activates the Iron Man source on his chest to create a gauntlet.

White fire shoots from the fingertips, and it burns through the metal locking devices. The doors swing open and there, sitting in pure, white light, is the Tesseract. Stark lifts it gently with the gauntlet and places it in his open case.

He allows himself a moment of satisfaction.

Then, a voice calls down the room, and Stark freezes. It is a familiar voice and one that he had really hoped *not* to hear during this time journey. Over recent years, Stark has developed a hard shell and an ability to forget the struggles of his past. This voice could melt all that.

The voice belongs to a handsome man in a suit who is carrying a bunch of flowers. "Hey! The door's this way!" he says with a friendly smile. "Do I know you?"

Stark walks toward him, but his legs feel strangely weak, and he nearly falls over a chair. He tries to avoid the man's eyes. "Er ... no. I'm a visitor, I'm ..." There is a slight tremble in his voice. "I'm ... Howard ... Howard ... Potts."

The other man laughs. "That's easy to remember!" he says. "I'm Howard *Stark*."

He offers his hand, and Stark reaches out to touch his father's fingers.

*This is so wrong, in so many ways*, Stark thinks as he walks out of the building with the man who gave him life. But something about the meeting also feels good. Stark, the scientist, enjoys the tricks that can result from playing with time, and he smiles.

Rogers is in Hank Pym's laboratory. It is a mess. Half-eaten sandwiches share space with wires and tubes of various different-colored liquids, reading glasses, jars, and papers.

He has only moments to take what they need. So many jars, bottles, and tubes. Where are they? He's looking for the same red tubes that have powered their time journeys until now. He turns and looks in cupboards, on shelves, on the tables among the papers and ... then, he smiles. At the end of the room is a glass case. Inside is a row of small, red tubes: the particles.

Within seconds, four of them are in Captain America's pocket, and he is out the door.

Howard Stark hands the flowers to Stark to hold while he straightens his tie.

"Got a date?" Stark asks his dad.

"No." Howard smiles. "My wife's expecting our first child."

"Ah—congratulations." Could things get any stranger? "I have a little girl," he tells his dad.

"Oh—I'd like a girl. There's less chance that she'll be like me." Howard smiles again.

*O.K. Maybe not so easy*, Rogers thought. Alarms are ringing and an officer who was with Rogers and Stark in the elevator is now calling for guards.

"There was something not quite right about them," she says.

Rogers opens the nearest door to hide and finds that time has taken him back not just physically, but emotionally, too. A picture of himself faces him from a shelf. Turning back to the door of the outer office, he reads the name *Margaret Carter*, and his heart starts to race. Peggy Carter! Of all the offices in the block, why has he chosen this one?

The face that he watches through the blinds on the windows separating the outer and inner rooms—older than he remembers but still beautiful—neither sees him nor senses his presence, and he can watch those familiar movements—the flick of her hair, the movement of her lips—for as long as he wants. He understands one thing very clearly; time has not changed him. Now he is seeing again the one person that he loved above all others, and the sight of her is cracking all the shields he has put up around his emotions. The present, the future, and the past have become one deep, unbelievable pain. Steve Rogers, Captain America, super hero, is unable to think or move.

"Tell me," Howard Stark asks. "Were you nervous? Did you feel ready?"

This was a side to his dad that Stark had never seen. Howard had been a strict, demanding father, but here was a guy who was unsure how to deal with a whole new way of life.

"There aren't any rules," Stark says. "My dad was strict with me, but now I just remember the good stuff. And he did give me some wise words." He paused and looked into his father's eyes. "Like 'No amount of money ever bought a second of time,'" he says, and waits for his dad's reaction.

"Smart guy," Howard finally says.

To the amazement of both men, Stark puts his arms around his dad's neck. "Thank you. For everything ...," and then he adds, "everything you've done for this country."

He walks across to Rogers, who has gone outside. Job done, in more ways than one.

### *Sanctuary II*, 2014

Nebula '23's whole body aches. Each time Nebula '14 delivers another kick or strikes her head on the metal floor, she is reminded of the way Thanos punished her as a child. But this time it is her own past self who is causing the suffering. She does not even try to fight back.

"You're weak," Nebula '14 whispers as she pulls back an arm and drags out another scream.

"I'm *you!*" says Nebula '23.

There is only disgust in Nebula '14's eyes. If this is what she becomes, she would rather die now. Then, her fingers touch a band on the outstretched wrist. She pulls it off and examines it closely, and smiles.

Gamora '14 looks at both sisters. Two Nebulas, from different times, and so completely different.

"You could stop all this." Nebula '23 looks directly into Gamora's eyes, when Nebula '14 leaves the room. "Thanos finds the Soul Stone," she says.

"Do you want to know how he does that?" She manages to pull herself to her knees. "You want to know what he does ... to you?" she asks. Her breath is shallow now ... Gamora must listen; she needs to know the part she plays in the future.

Gamora's eyes do not change expression.

"Enough." Nebula '14 returns and kicks Nebula '23 onto her back. Her left hand shoots out, closes tightly around the throat, and pulls their heads together. "You disgust me. But that doesn't mean you're useless."

Then, light flashes silver from the knife she is holding in her right hand. The shining edge slides across Nebula '23's cheek and pauses for a moment under her left eye. Then, it moves upward to the gold, metal plate above it. The point enters where the metal sections join and carefully lifts the one that is of interest. Nebula' 14 removes the gold plate very gently; not to spare pain, but to keep it undamaged.

**The shining edge slides across Nebula '23's cheek and pauses for a moment under her left eye.**

Nebula '14 kneels in front of Thanos and places a small, red tube in his great hand. It contains the Pym Particles. Then, she lifts her head. The gold plate is fixed in place.

"How do I look?" she asks.

### Vormir, 2014

Vormir is a strange, silent planet. There is no day, no night, just continual deep shadow, broken only by occasional waves of purple light on the oily lakes. Barton and Natasha start their hunt for the Soul Stone. A mountain rises from the flat land, with two dark, rocky fingers pointing toward the clouded sky.

It is a hard climb. Snow makes the stone paths icy, and it blinds them as they struggle upward.

"Welcome!" The word floats in the air like a dying breath.

The two Avengers turn, Natasha's gun and Barton's sword aiming at the source of the voice. Moving waves of deeper shadows form a constantly changing shape in front of them. It has no substance, like smoke.

"Natasha, daughter of Ivan." The voice drifts like the shadows it speaks from. "Clint, son of Edith."

Ice touches the back of Natasha's neck. Not even *she* knows her father's name. "Who are you?" she demands.

The shadows move slightly, and for a moment the edge of red bones where a face should be, and an inky, deep blackness that perhaps held eyes, appear. Then, the shadows drift again, and whatever has been uncovered disappears again into the smoke.

"Think of me as a guide," it breathes. "To you, and all who search for the Soul Stone."

Natasha lifts her chin. "Good," she says. "You tell us where it is, and we'll go."

The shadowy figure's voice rises a little, and its words carry a soft threat. "It is not so easy."

The shape drifts forward and, following it with weapons still raised, the

Avengers find themselves at the top of a tall, steep tower of rock. They are on the edge, and below them there seems to be no end to the darkness. It feels like a window to hell, and they are looking into its depths.

A low sun burns gold behind the tower and colors the rising smoke pink, but it only makes the blackness below even darker. It offers no hope, no real brightness.

"The object that you are looking for lies in front of you," their dark guide whispers. "And also, your greatest fear."

Natasha stares down into the emptiness. "The Stone is down there." She knows that the end of their adventure is close.

"For *one* of you." The words carry clearly in the cold air. They are familiar words for this shadowy shape; they have been repeated many times to many searchers. "To take the Stone, you must lose that which you love. A soul for a soul. An exchange that will last for all time."

"Perhaps this is just one big lie," Barton suggests, but Natasha knows it is true.

"Thanos left here without his daughter," she reminds him quietly. "Why?"

The Avengers look at each other. They have been best friends for a very long time. Now, they need to make a choice, to give one of their lives to save millions of people. One of them will die. The other will lose their friend—which will also be like a death.

Barton half smiles. For him, the choice is obvious. "Yeah. Then I guess we both know who it's got to be." He takes her hand in his.

"I guess we do," Natasha agrees and covers his hand with her own. As they look at each other, Barton realizes that Natasha has made her own choice.

"You know me better than anyone, Clint." Her voice is faint. "For five years, all I've been aiming for is *this*—to be here, to bring everyone back."

"No." Barton shakes his head. Natasha is still needed by so many people. "You know what I've become." His shame is clear. "For five years, I've been a killer. I can't live with that, Natasha. I want to do this. I *need* to do this."

But Natasha's face is like stone. Yes, Barton has done evil things, but she forgives him. His family will return, and he will change. This is now *her* decision, *her* life to give. The soul to be exchanged must be hers.

*She's right about one thing*, Barton thinks, *I know her better than anyone. She will not change her mind about this final action.*

"O.K.," he says softly.

They touch foreheads, neither wanting to let the other see the tears in their eyes, and they hold on to this last moment for as long as they can. The sun is shining pink behind the tower, and snow catches in their hair. The guide watches and waits.

Then, Barton pulls back. "You win," he smiles.

And then he kicks her knee, and when she falls he holds her down. "Tell my family I love them," he says.

But Natasha is prepared and throws him off. She stands and stretches out her hand toward him—not to help him up, but to activate her Black Widow's bracelet.

"You tell them yourself!" she cries, and blue fire shoots from her wrist, hitting Barton in the chest. The electricity pulses through his body, freezing his arms and legs.

Black Widow turns and stares at the emptiness beyond the edge of the tower. Then, head down, she runs full speed toward it. But before she gets close, Barton is back on his feet—Hawkeye now—and reaching for an arrow. He shoots, and the force of the small explosion knocks Black Widow to the ground. With no hesitation, Hawkeye runs past her, reaches the edge, and leaps out into the icy air. For a moment, he hangs,

weightless, his mind finally clear, the last years wiped away. He has done it. He is falling.

Until ... he suddenly crashes hard into the side of the tower.

What has stopped his fall? A tree, a branch, a rock? No, a body. Black Widow's body. She has leaped after him, shot a line of metal to hook them to the rocky edge of the tower, and snapped the end of the line to his waist. They are both hanging there, between the icy safety of the rock above and the death waiting in the dark below. But it is Black Widow whose eyes are the clearest, the brightest. She has control. Desperate, Hawkeye holds tightly to her wrist, but his friend's fingers do not even try to close around his hand. She is slipping away from him.

"Please," he begs her.

Black Widow's face is calm as she looks up at him for the last time. She can feel the shadows and the Soul Stone pulling her down.

"It's O.K.," she says.

She pushes away from the tower wall, away from Hawkeye's hand, and drops into the darkness.

Hawkeye's eyes follow her fall until he has to turn away. But he knows when she dies. The whole atmosphere explodes. Shining blue lights surge upward from the rocky fingers, burning into the heavy clouds, and lightning and thunder crash around the tower.

Hawkeye's mind flashes white, and then he loses consciousness.

They touch foreheads, neither wanting to let the other see the tears in their eyes ...

When his eyes open, he is lying on his back in the oily waters of a lake, comfortably calm. Then, his heart contracts violently and he kneels, unsure where he is or how he got there.

He is alone. In the cold. In the dark.

But not completely alone; there is something in the protective glove that covers his hand. He opens his fingers, and the bright orange of the Soul Stone shines up at him. The memories flood back. It has happened. The exchange has been made. Natasha's soul for the Soul Stone. Clint Barton cries for the past and the future.

**When his eyes open, he is lying on his back in the oily waters of a lake, comfortably calm.**

# Return to the Future

With their senses shut down by the speed of the return journey, the teams of time travelers raced through the quantum world completely unconscious of the colors and tunnels they were blasting through. All they experienced was a bright, blue flash after flicking their time bands. Then, a wonder and exhaustion filled their minds and bodies when their suit helmets opened; they were standing in the same circle that they had left—it seemed years ago, but in real time, it was just a few minutes.

They looked around them. Had they done the impossible? Had they returned with all six Stones?

Hulk spoke first. "Did we get them all?" He looked around the group. Satisfaction and excitement shone on every face. On every face apart from one: Barton's.

The excitement immediately disappeared. There was complete silence. No breathing, no heartbeats as they realized that Natasha's place was empty. Hulk hit the platform floor with a wordless anger.

Thor couldn't understand. "You're acting like she's dead. She's *not* dead. We have the Stones!" He faced Barton. "We can bring her back."

"No, we can't." Barton knew what he had seen, what had been said, what his friend had died for. "It cannot be changed." It was an inevitability.

No power, not even the Stones, could change that.

Hulk threw a table across the room. He was both sad and angry. "We have to make it worth it."

"We will." Rogers's voice was hard. He could not believe that one of his greatest friends was gone forever. He would never see her lovely smile or hear her voice again. But they, the Avengers, would make Thanos pay for her death. He was sure about that.

The next part of the plan was dangerous. They had all six Stones, but each one needed to be carefully placed in position in a new Infinity Gauntlet. This would capture the power of all the Stones, bring them together, and allow the Avengers to undo Thanos's actions—this time, bringing back the disappeared. But each Stone had enormous strength and the power to damage whoever held it. It would be extremely dangerous for one person to hold all six Stones.

First, Stark designed a new gauntlet and then, from behind a protective screen, he carefully used small mechanical arms to move each Stone into its correct place. When the final Stone, the Soul Stone, was in place, the gauntlet shone red and gold. It was done. Stark then used another device to hold the gauntlet in the air, ready for someone's hand. The question was—who would put it on?

"It has to be me!" Thor argued. He was the strongest; he was the only one able to take the gauntlet's power. He was a god. "It's my duty!"

"No." Stark was firm. "We need to discuss this."

Thor looked into Stark's eyes. "Please," he begged. "I *need* to do this.

Let me just do this one thing right. Please!"

Stark gently shook his head. "There is enough power in that gauntlet to light up a whole continent!" he said. "And you're not in the best physical shape."

"It has to be *me*." Hulk walked forward and stared at the gauntlet. "You all saw what this did to Thanos. None of you could live through it." He paused. "But *I* might. My powers now are all the result of gamma rays. The Infinity Stones' power is from gamma rays, and my body can take them. I was *made* for this."

One member of the team didn't get involved in the argument: Nebula. She had wandered back into the room with the Quantum Tunnel. There, when she was sure that she was unobserved, she removed the glove from the hand that had been burned by taking the Stone on Morag. But the hand was perfect. *This* hand had never held the Power Stone, because this was not Nebula '23. It was Nebula '14. She had used the time wristband to travel forward in time, to help her father, to finally gain his respect.

Now, she put her metal fingers inside the tunnel controls and set new calculations. She flicked a switch and waited for a portal to open that would allow *Sanctuary II* through to 2023.

"Remember, Bruce, you're only bringing the *people* back. Don't change anything else from the last five years," Stark said.

Hulk approached the gauntlet and lifted his hand.

In a circle around him, the Avengers had their weapons: Captain America held his shield; War Machine and Iron Man activated their helmets; Hawkeye was ready with his bow; Ant-Man's suit closed around him; Rocket had his gun; and Thor's hand was stretched out ready—for his ax, Stormbreaker, or his hammer, Mjolnir. No one noticed Nebula's absence.

Lightning streamed from each stone, their different colors combining to create one pure, white power source that surged into Hulk's arm.

Shields closed over windows and doors. Nothing could get in or out of the Avengers building. It was time.

Hulk watched the last door close. He breathed deeply. "Everybody comes home," he whispered, and slowly put his fingers into the gauntlet. The red metal shone brightly and grew larger to close completely around the big man's wrist, hand, and fingers. Then, the Stones flashed into life.

Lightning streamed from each Stone, their different colors combining to create one pure, white power source that surged into Hulk's arm. He screamed and dropped to his knees. The electricity pulsed through his arms, across his shoulders, into his chest, and he roared with the pain. He threw back his head as the power blasted through him, again and again. His eyes shut. His throat closed. His hands froze. The gauntlet burned and burned.

"Take it off!" Thor cried. The gauntlet was killing the big man.

"Are you O.K.?" Captain America shouted over the noise. "Talk to me!"

Hulk finally managed to move his head. "Yes." His body was boiling with different energies, but his reaction to the gamma rays was controlling the power.

Nebula flicked more switches and the metal circles above the tunnel platform started to turn and spin. She smiled. Inside the tunnel, her father's spaceship, a tiny spot of red light, raced through time. The platform opened wide and *Sanctuary II* roared through the spinning circles of gold, growing larger and larger, until—like an enormous metal bird—it burst out through the glass roof of the building into the sky. Thanos had arrived in 2023. And Nebula kept the portal open.

Fighting the pain and the force of the energy that was pulsing through him, Hulk used his left hand to try to force the gauntlet fingers together. He needed all his strength, as the gauntlet pushed back against him each time. The colored fires burned brighter and brighter, and he screamed with the effort. But then, finally, a finger touched his thumb and ... snap! It was done.

The Stones lost their fire; the power in Hulk's body died, and the big man fell unconscious on the floor.

Thor immediately kicked away the gauntlet, and Iron Man cooled Hulk's skin with jets of water from his battle-suited fingers. The whole arm was a mess of burns. The big man opened his eyes. "Did we do it?" he asked.

The metal doors lifted, and Hawkeye cautiously went through. Everywhere was silent, and he found himself holding his breath. Then, he heard a faint *buzz*, and he realized that it was his phone on the table. The face on the screen was Laura, his wife. Hawkeye froze. Could it be? He answered it, and a voice he had not heard for five years said, "Clint?"

Ant-Man looked out the window. Birds were singing; the air seemed to have a different quality. He turned to the others. "Guys," he said, "I think we did it."

For a moment, lying on his back on the floor, Hulk felt his whole body relax. He looked up through the glass roof at the blue sky. It was O.K. They had gone through hell, but they had come out again. They had done the impossible.

Then, he saw the tip of a bird's wing crossing the sky. As he watched, it grew into an enormous dark shadow that took all the light from the glass window. It was not a bird.

It was *Sanctuary II*, from 2014.

Stunned, Hulk saw the first ball of white flame crash through the glass above him, and as he rolled away, the floor exploded. Bomb after bomb rained down on the building, destroying metal, glass, wood, anything in their paths, throwing up enormous clouds of black smoke. Thanos had no hesitation. How dare these creatures question his actions? Within seconds, the ground below him was burned black and the buildings were ruins; dust-filled smoke drifted across the piles of stones and bricks.

There had been no time to react. The first shock threw the Avengers off their feet. The following bombs found their targets and crashed through floor after floor, sending some of them sliding down to the depths of the building, crushing others under rocks and stones. The smoke was blinding, and water roared through broken pipes into the newly created underground caves.

In one of these, Hulk was using all his strength to prevent a heavy, metal bar from crashing down on his friends Rocket and Rhodey.

"I can't hold it much longer!" he shouted.

But Rocket couldn't move. War Machine used a metal pole to free him, but more water thundered into the cave, filling it up fast.

"Help! Help! Can anyone hear?" War Machine shouted into his communication device. "Three of us, lowest level. Water's coming in!"

Ant-Man was on the top of a pile of stones, shaking dust from his head and the fog from his brain. He was tiny again. He heard the call.

"Wait!" he cried. "I'm down here, too. I'm coming!"

Hawkeye got to his knees and looked around. His heart was racing, but he seemed to be unhurt. What had happened? Where was everyone? Were they even alive? Low, red emergency lights showed him that he was trapped in one of the underground pipe tunnels. With his head bent, he walked a few steps, his flashlight showing him the bricks and stones ahead. There were open holes in parts of the roof where it had fallen, and there was broken rock everywhere. Then, the light found something caught between two rocks on the tunnel floor. He could hardly believe it. After all the bombing and destruction, the Infinity Gauntlet had landed at his feet.

Suddenly, the hairs on the back of his neck trembled. He stood completely still and listened, and then he heard it: a scratching sound. Hawkeye pulled out an arrow and aimed his bow back along the tunnel. The scratching increased, but he still had no sense of what it was. He let the arrow fly, and as it traveled, it lit up the tunnel. The tunnel was full of creatures, running along the floor, up the walls, along the ceilings. Outriders—Thanos's creatures that had helped the Titan attack the Avengers in Wakanda.

*O.K.*, he thought. *Time to go.* He picked up the gauntlet and ran for his life.

Thanos stood in the center of the destruction he had caused. Nebula '14 walked confidently toward her father through the drifting smoke.

"Well done, daughter," he said, and her heart filled with pride.

He placed his enormous sword in the ground and put his battle helmet on top. Then, he sat.

"Go. Find me the Stones," he ordered.

From *Sanctuary II,* spread in the sky like a great shadow over the ruins below, Gamora '14 looked down at the horror her father had brought, and Nebula '23 realized how she had unknowingly brought the world to this point.

Gamora needed answers, now. "What happens to you and me in the future?" she asked her sister.

Nebula looked up. "I will try to kill you," she said simply. "Many times." She paused slightly. "And then, we will become friends ... sisters."

There was a place in Gamora's heart that had always hoped for this, but it had been crushed time after time by their father's demands. Was this new Nebula right? Could there be the faint chance of a friendship between them, and the possibility of a future free of destruction? She stretched out a hand and helped her sister to stand.

"Come on," Gamora said. "Together, we can stop him."

**Thanos stood in the center of the destruction he had caused.**

# Forces Unite

Stark was shaken but—amazingly—unhurt in the remains of his laboratory. Everything was broken, burned, or burning, and the air was bitter with the smell of smoke. What had happened? Had their use of the gauntlet achieved the opposite of what they had intended? Was he the only one alive? Scared of what he might find, he walked across the cracked floor and brushed away the ropes of black wires hanging down. Then, he saw a flash of white and red under some stones: Captain America's shield.

Stark pulled at his friend's arm. "Wake up!" he whispered.

Finally, Rogers opened his eyes. He looked around the black shell of the building in confusion. "Did the Stones do this?" he asked, in disbelief.

"Who knows?" Stark said quietly. "If you play games with time, it can play games with you."

He helped Rogers stand, and then, through the smoke, they saw a familiar, dark shape. Thor was standing, looking out across the ruined buildings. The whole area was dark with dust and smoke: the sky, the air, the ground. Small fires were still burning and creating strange dancing shadows.

At the center of the darkness, Thanos sat. He seemed to be made of stone. The metal of his battle suit shone dirty gold in the light of the fires.

"He hasn't moved," Thor said quietly. "You know it's a trap."

Stark's voice was dead. "I don't much care," he replied.

Thor gave a small smile. "Then, if we are all agreed ..."

His eyes narrowed and flashed blue. In the depths of the dark clouds above them, thunder cracked open the sky, and Thor lifted his arms. Lightning shot down into his open hands and fire flowed through him, branching and twisting blue lines through his whole body. His eyes now burned white, and the electricity shooting around him brought his weapons, Stormbreaker and Mjolnir, to his hands.

"Let's kill him properly this time," the God of Thunder said.

The three Avengers prepared: their weapons were ready and their senses were sharp. The Titan watched them approach. No movement, no fear, no expression.

"You could not live with your failure," he said, almost softly, almost sadly. "And now ..." There was a slight smile. "Now, it has brought you back to me. I had hoped that by killing half the creatures in the universe, the other half would grow and lead better lives. You have shown me that I was wrong."

His voice was slow and calm; his reasoning was like that of someone wise and ancient, but his words were terrifying.

He stood up, his great size towering over the three Avengers. "While there are people living who still remember the past, they will never be able to move forward. I thank you. Now I know what I must do." He lifted his helmet from the enormous sword and slowly put it on—a soldier, preparing carefully for a battle. Then, he looked at them, and his voice held a terrible promise. Each word cut through the air like a bullet. "I shall destroy every atom of this universe. Then, with the Stones you have collected for me, I shall create a new one. A universe full of life that doesn't know what it has lost; only what it has been given. A *grateful* universe."

"A universe born out of blood," Captain America cried.

"But they will never know it," Thanos continued, and raised his double-bladed sword, "because you will not be alive to tell them."

Then, Thor roared—a roar full of guilt and shame; a roar that powered both the ax and the hammer as he leaped into the air; a roar that called

Iron Man and Captain America into battle beside him. Iron Man's metal gloves blasted fire, and Captain America's shield rang with the blows from Thanos's sword. The fight had begun.

Underground, in the air pocket, more and more water poured into the small space. The surging waters had nearly reached the roof, and Rocket could smell and taste the closeness of death.

Then, the voice came again. "I'm coming!"

Ant-Man was riding the waves of the flowing water on a tiny piece of wood. He was getting closer.

Hawkeye ran like the wind. The tunnel behind him was full of Outriders— he could hear their bodies scratching and sliding; the air was thick with their smell. He paused to set a trap with three arrows, placed carefully in three pipes. Then, he ran again. Behind him the arrows exploded, creating a ball of flames. The Outriders' screams cut through the roar of the fire, but Hawkeye could not stop even to take a breath. More creatures were climbing over the dead ones, and he could feel the heat from the fireball at his back. Then, he saw a hole that had opened in the tunnel roof. He shot a line upward, through a channel, to hook into the rocky wall of a room above. As he was pulled up, Outriders leaped at his feet and tried to drag him down, but his sword flashed, cutting and slicing at them, until finally, he lay exhausted on the floor of the room, with the Infinity Gauntlet beside him. The sounds of the Outriders were gone. For the moment, he was safe.

But he was not alone. A familiar figure, gray and blue face now bathed in red light, reached down to lift the heavy gauntlet. Hawkeye relaxed. He was not the only one left alive. Nebula was there, too. And if she was alive, the others might be.

"Father, I have the Stones."

Nebula '14's whispered voice into her communication device killed Hawkeye's moment of calm in a second. *What?* The Avenger struggled to sit up, but a metal foot on his chest prevented him from moving. Nebula pointed her gun at his head.

"Stop!" A green-skinned woman entered the room, and she was followed by ... another Nebula. Hawkeye closed his eyes. Was he seeing double? Had he damaged his eyes? But no, there were still two Nebulas when he reopened them.

Slowly, he understood. This must be Gamora, Nebula's sister, and somehow, Nebula from the past had taken the place of the Nebula of the Avengers team. She had brought Thanos through the Quantum Tunnel to fight for the Stones again.

Nebula '14 lifted her boot to balance herself better and redirect her gun toward the other Nebula. Hawkeye rolled away.

"No!" Gamora '14 shouted to her sister from the past. "Don't do this! You can change—you *do* change!"

For a moment, Gamora saw a deep, deep sadness in her sister's dark eyes. There was an emptiness there, too: a complete absence of hope. "He won't let me," Nebula '14 said simply. Then, she turned her gun to Gamora.

The noise of the shot rocketed around the room, but it wasn't Gamora who was hit. Nebula '14 fell against the wall, her hand over a hole blasted in her chest. She took a final breath, and as she looked into her killer's eyes, her expression was calm. Perhaps her twisted brain had found peace at last and was grateful to her older self, Nebula '23, for ending everything.

Hawkeye picked up the Infinity Gauntlet.

There was a battle to fight.

Above ground, the three Avengers were in trouble.

"Thor, hit me!" Iron Man cried from the air.

Pulling down lightning again, Thor created an enormous electrical surge by crashing his weapons together, and shot it to Iron Man. The surge super-energized Iron Man's suit and blasters. The power that now rained down on Thanos was beyond imagination. But the Titan just smiled and spun his sword in faster circles, redirecting every hit.

The hammer was next. Thor sent it screaming blue lightning through the air, but Thanos threw Iron Man in its path, like a toy. Mjolnir struck the Avenger with the power of an exploding bomb, and the great Avenger was down, on his back, with the full force of Thor's energy still racing through his suit and body. Iron Man's eyes closed.

Two Avengers were still standing. Thor was the first to fall. The Titan knocked Stormbreaker away with ease and rained blow after violent blow down on the god until he couldn't move; pain streamed through his whole body. He could not call down the lightning, his weapons were useless, but ... there was still feeling in his fingers. Slowly, he lifted part of a damaged hand, and his dry lips smiled through the blood. Stormbreaker trembled on the ground and then rose to its master's call; it flew directly toward him.

But Thanos's reactions were quicker than ever. He shot out his own arm, caught the flying ax, and immediately attacked the god himself with it. The Titan pressed the weapon down, closer and closer, and Thor was nearer to death than he had ever been, and from his *own* weapon. But it was not his only one. With the power of the god's mind alone, Mjolnir moved on the ground, heavily at first, then it surged into the air and flew toward its target—not Thor's weak hand, but Thanos's head. The Titan's shoulders cracked back, and he lost hold of the ax. Mjolnir's flight then curled back toward another hand that reached out for it. Through his pain, Thor smiled again. It was Captain America who now held the hammer, showing, at last, that there was another person in the world who was worthy.

"I knew it," Thor whispered.

Thanos's metal gauntlet struck the God of Thunder one last time—a blow full of the power of centuries of hatred—and the light in Thor's eyes faded. He could do no more.

Channeling all Mjolnir's power, the last Avenger standing leaped at Thanos and struck him with Thor's hammer again and again, sending powerful, blue electricity through the big man every time, but Thanos answered each attack; his double blades swung again and again. Finally, Thanos forced the hammer from Captain America's hands ... and concentrated on the shield. The enormous blade struck the shield again and again, driving the Avenger backward. And eventually, the unimaginable happened: the shield cracked, and split.

Captain America lay on the black earth, unable to breathe, too weak to rise again. As his eyes clouded over, he stared up at the great shadow of *Sanctuary II* above them. They had failed. Completely. Perhaps inevitably. They had not only failed to bring back the disappeared, but their efforts had led to the destruction of the rest of the universe. The Titan had won. There was no hope left.

Thanos looked down at the little man with his broken shield. "In all my years of battle, of violence, of death, it was never personal." He spoke quietly, almost to himself. "I had an aim and I worked toward that." He paused for a moment, and a cold light flashed in his eyes. "But I'll tell you now. I have plans for this annoying little planet of yours ... and I'm going to enjoy them very, very much."

As the Avenger watched, blue beams powered down from *Sanctuary II*, creating a pale mist over the dark ruins, and a line of familiar shapes

It was Captain America who now held the hammer, showing, at last, that there was another person in the world who was worthy.

stood in the evil light. Captain America recognized them all; they were creatures from the worst dreams of the past—the Children of Thanos. He saw Ebony Maw, Proxima Midnight, and behind them, pouring through the time portal that Nebula '14 had held open, came Outriders, Chitauri, and Leviathans, enormous creatures used by the Chitauri as warships. They came, more and more, out of the darkness. There was no end to the army of the most dangerous servants of evil in the universe.

Captain America struggled to stand. He held the cracked remains of his shield in front of him, and faced Thanos and his army of terror. He was one man against thousands, but this one Avenger represented all those that Thanos had killed, turned to dust, and terrified. This one man would not stop fighting until the last breath had left his body. He held his head high.

And then, the impossible happened.

"Cap?" A small voice spoke in his communication device. It was the voice of Sam Wilson—Falcon—one of the disappeared. "On your left!"

Captain America looked. He could not believe what he was seeing. Was it a trick of the light? A small, gold circle was spinning in the dark sky. No, not a trick. Slowly, the circle grew larger and larger, and sank to sit low in the sky like an enormous, shining sun. Figures stepped forward through the light. He saw Black Panther, Shuri, and Okoye from Wakanda; their backs were straight, their spears were raised.

The Avenger's heart started to race.

More golden circles, small and large, appeared in the darkness. Through one flew Valkyrie on a winged horse; through another floated the sorcerer, Doctor Strange and his assistant, Wong. Another opened and several of the Guardians of the Galaxy leaped out: Star-Lord in front, followed by

Drax, Mantis, and Groot. A suited figure jumped through another circle: it was Spider-Man.

Captain America could not speak or move.

They had done it.

The Stones had brought everyone back. Over there was Scarlet Witch, and in other circles were Winter Soldier and The Wasp. Beyond her was Falcon ... And then, the black earth cracked open, and an enormous shape burst through and rose into the sky. Ant-Man, grown taller than ever before, opened his hands and Rocket, Hulk, and War Machine were with him. Stark's wife, Pepper Potts, arrived in her own iron suit.

Armies followed through the gold portals, from every part of the universe: Wakandans, Ravagers, sorcerers, Asgardians. Thousands of voices cheered, Wakandan spears hit the ground, magical hands spun circles of gold.

The electric atmosphere touched Thor, and his eyes opened. The God of Thunder's heart trembled, and he struggled to his feet with Stormbreaker in his hand. Iron Man's eyes opened, too, in wonder and disbelief. FRIDAY had repaired his damaged suit and body; he was ready again for battle. For the final fight.

The Avengers stood together, and this time they were not alone. Everything they had ever done, every life saved, every enemy defeated, and every lesson learned had brought them to this point.

Captain America looked around at the forces of good that had come to fight for their world, and he looked at Thanos with his creatures, who had been called to destroy it.

"Avengers, assemble!" Captain America cried.

There was a great roar.

More golden circles, small and large, appeared in the darkness.

# The Endgame

Thanos watched, expressionless, as the armies grouped in front of him. Then, he lowered his blade and pointed. It gave his dark forces the signal they wanted to begin the attack on their enemy. Roars filled the air, and the ground shook, as they surged toward the creatures that they had been designed to destroy. On the ground and in the air, the armies crashed into each other with spears, swords, teeth, and guns. Blasters burned wings and cut into metal; blue and bright orange energy sent fire and death; spaceships burst into flames; small figures with simple knives attacked enormous creatures covered in heavy metal.

Every hero used his or her power. Spinning gold circles threw attackers back; spears sliced and killed with quiet efficiency, and Ant-Man's enormous feet crushed everything underfoot as he marched across the enemy army. The whole battlefield was full of fire and blood, and the constant shooting, screaming, shouting, and crashing was a thunderous wall of sound. Air, previously thick with smoke and dust, was now filled with fear, pain, and death.

And in the middle of the enormous battle, there were moments of joy.

Iron Man turned to come face to face with the boy who had given him the courage to start this whole daring plan: Spider-Man.

"You will not believe what's been happening!" The boy's words streamed out of his mouth excitedly. "Remember when we were in space, and there was all that dust? I think I lost consciousness, and you were gone, but then Doctor Strange was there, and he said, 'It's been five years. Let's go. They need us ...'"

Iron Man put his arms around the young super hero, who was filled with happiness to see his friend again. "Oh, this is nice," he smiled.

Star-Lord was having a really great time. Every enemy he shot or kicked went down, but his luck almost ended when he found himself facing a Chitauri sword and unable to move. *Oof!* The Chitauri's body landed on top of him, killed by a blaster. Unfolding himself from the body, the Guardian's heart jumped. His rescuer was Gamora, his friend, his love.

"I thought I lost you!" Tenderly, he touched the cheek of the person he had thought he would never see again.

And Gamora '14 kicked him. Hard. "Don't touch me!" she warned. Then, she looked across at Nebula '23, doubt on her face. "This?" She pointed in disgust at Quill, his face screwed up in pain on the ground. "*This* is the one? Seriously?" she asked.

Nebula lifted her shoulders. "Your choices were him or ...," she pointed at Groot, "... a tree."

On another part of the battlefield, Hawkeye was still protecting the Infinity Gauntlet. He ran, but where to? What could he do with it? Where should he take it? They needed to return the Stones to their original places in time, to protect their futures. But how?

"We can use Pym's van tunnel again," Ant-Man shouted over the communication device. He pulled out his phone, pressed a button, and a car alarm sounded in the distance. He and The Wasp became tiny, and flew toward the ugly little van.

But Hawkeye was being attacked on every side for what he carried. His arrows and fire helped, but there were too many attackers. Then, just in time, Black Panther appeared above him, and Hawkeye threw him the gauntlet. Immediately, the creatures turned to follow *him*, striking him with fire and bullets again and again. The King of Wakanda just smiled; his special suit stored all the energy that it received, and when he later struck the ground with his hand, he returned all the force, destroying everything around him.

Then, Thanos's blade caught him and the gauntlet was thrown into the air. This time it was Scarlet Witch's turn. She stood between Thanos and his prize. Her magical, red beams of energy crushed the Titan between two enormous rocks and then lifted him into the air, sending continual pulses of red fire through him.

Black Panther ran for the gauntlet, but saw it rise magically, controlled by Ebony Maw. He leaped and held it again, but was kept in the air by Ebony Maw's force.

"I got it!" Spider-Man was close, and Black Panther passed the gauntlet to him. The boy sped away.

Thanos felt his life energy being destroyed by Scarlet Witch's unbelievable power. There was one final answer: "Destroy! Send down all our power!" he screamed at *Sanctuary II*. Both armies would suffer with the full power of *Sanctuary II*'s weapons, but he didn't care. He needed to live; he needed to use the Stones.

Evil creatures—whether they were flying, running, or leaping—were struck by the powerful beams of fire from the ship. Doctor Strange's band of sorcerers spun gold, protective shields above the heads of their own armies, but in spite of this, Ravagers, Wakandans, and Asgardians were also struck by the continual attacks from the sky.

And the gauntlet was still in danger. Spider-Man held it close, but Outriders and Chitauri were climbing all over him. "I'm O.K.!" he cried— then, "I'm *not* O.K. Help! Someone, help!"

"Here!" Captain America shouted and threw Thor's hammer. Spider-Man reached for the flying weapon and was pulled out of the pile of creatures. Boldly, he flew onward with the gauntlet until he was knocked back to the ground. Blasts from *Sanctuary II* filled the air with clouds of rocks and stones, metal and blood; it was impossible to see through the dark fog and to know where to run to. Spider-Man curled into a tight ball, protecting the Stones and closing his ears against the screaming and roaring of the bombs, fire, and explosions.

Then, suddenly, the bombs stopped falling.

All on the battlefield raised their eyes. *Sanctuary II* had turned its blue, destructive beams toward space, reaching out into the blackness. But why? The reason suddenly became clear. A gold ball of fire powered like a rocket through all the beams and into the enormous spaceship, leaving explosion after explosion behind it. The whole ship burst into flames and slowly broke apart, the burning metal crashing down onto the battlefield.

The golden fireball became a shining, human form and landed beside Spider-Man. Captain Marvel smiled, and Spider-Man passed her the gauntlet for the last stage of its journey to the Quantum Tunnel.

Avengers and heroes cleared a path for the gauntlet through the enemy fire, and Captain Marvel sped like an arrow toward the van. Thanos was waiting, but she knocked him back with a beam of enormous power. The Titan thought quickly, turned, and threw his remaining blade at the van itself. A clever decision, from one of the smartest minds in the universe.

The whole ship burst into flames and slowly broke apart ...

The blade hit its target, and the Quantum Tunnel exploded. Shock waves spread out across an enormous area; the ground trembled; creatures and heroes were thrown into the air by the enormous blast of wind and energy.

Captain Marvel dropped the gauntlet.

And Thanos ran for it.

But there were three Avengers close to it: Iron Man, Thor, and Captain America. All were battle tired, but all knew that this was the endgame. And so, the last struggle for the Stones began—as the whole fight had begun—in the black ruins of the Avengers' building, a lifetime ago now. At that time, the three of them had proved no match for the Titan's superhuman strength. And nothing had changed.

Exhausted and hardly able to stand, the Avengers watched with sinking hearts as Thanos lifted the Infinity Gauntlet. Was there one more chance? Captain Marvel flew directly at the Titan and struggled to take the gauntlet, but Thanos was so close to his dream now that his strength appeared to double and he knocked her away. As she lay, breathless, he put his hand inside the gauntlet. The Stones came alive, and their energy pulled a great roar from him, full of both unbearable pain and limitless power. He lifted the Infinity Gauntlet to the sky.

And brought his finger and thumb together.

But not completely. Captain Marvel leaped at him again, and with every part of her body shining with energy she held onto his raised fingers. All her power was concentrated on those fingers, keeping them apart. The two powers were matched. Their strength was equal. Thanos realized that he could not win. So, with his other hand, he slowly reached across to the gauntlet and picked out one Stone, the Power Stone. He closed his fingers around it and pulled back the hand to strike. He looked into Captain Marvel's eyes and hit her with the full power of the Stone. She was thrown into the air.

Thanos put the Power Stone back in the gauntlet and lifted his arm again. No one could stop him now. He had defeated every Avenger. He had lost his evil armies and he was alone, but he needed nobody, nothing, apart from this gauntlet and these living Stones. This was the moment.

**Almost knowing what he would see, Thanos turned the gauntlet over. There were empty spaces where the Stones had been.**

Now he could achieve his ambition: to destroy the universe and rebuild it to his own design.

The world seemed to stop, and every living being on the battlefield turned toward that one place. But Iron Man was looking at Doctor Strange, who was holding back a threatening flood of waters. The Avenger's eyes held a question, and Strange answered it by lifting one finger. One. When, so long ago, he had been forced to give Thanos the Time Stone, to save Iron Man's life, he had calculated their success of beating Thanos: one chance in fourteen million. This was it.

Iron Man was physically as weak as he had ever been, but his brain was still working. He ran toward the Titan, and his fingers closed around the gauntlet, pulling as hard as he could—but he was brushed away like an annoying insect, as he had expected.

Thanos raised the Infinity Gauntlet again for the last time. He looked around at all the death and destruction and smiled. His dream. They had tried to stop him, but it was impossible.

"I ... am ... inevitable," Thanos said, victory in his eyes and voice, and he snapped his fingers.

Nothing happened.

Nothing changed.

The dark world was still dark. Bodies lay where they had fallen. There was no dust.

Almost knowing what he would see, Thanos turned the gauntlet over. There were empty spaces where the Stones had been.

Then, he looked at Iron Man, lying, physically broken, where Thanos had thrown him. The Avenger's eyes were unbearably tired, full of pain and fearful of the inevitability of what was going to happen next. But the power of life and death for the whole universe now rested in one of his hands.

He raised it.

Iron Man's own Infinity Gauntlet was now alive with the bright, shining colors of the six Infinity Stones. He had taken them during his seemingly weak effort to pull the gauntlet from Thanos. The Stones' energy powered down his arm, bright colors spreading through his body, the pain forcing his head back, closing his throat.

"And … I …" Iron Man's voice was weak as he fought the power of the Stones, but hatred gave him the words, "… am … Iron … Man!"

He stared at Thanos, angrily, bitterly. He forced down the pain, and with his eyes still fixed on Thanos, he snapped his fingers.

The world went white.

And the air changed. A strange electricity spread across the battlefield. It touched dust-darkened faces, cooled wounds, and lifted defeated heads. And it brought a pale lightness into the dark, as great flying Leviathans and ships dropped from the sky, ghosts of black smoke.

**Iron Man's own Infinity Gauntlet was now alive with the bright, shining colors of the six Infinity Stones.**

Thanos watched as the remains of his armies became dust. Ebony Maw's features clouded and faded into the wind; creatures melted; all the dark dust was taken up into the air. And like an enormous wave of flying insects it grouped, regrouped, and finally disappeared. The sun was rising; the sky was alive again with color and hope.

Thanos, the enormous, powerful destroyer, slowly sat down. And as his dreams turned to dust, so did he.

Iron Man fell back against a rock. His face was empty; his staring eyes looked dead. Blood and burns covered his skin.

"You did it, Mr. Stark." Peter Parker touched the dying man's shoulder. "You *did* it. We won!" Tears started to fall.

Pepper knelt in front of her husband. They looked at each other, and Stark tried to make his lips smile. Pepper closed her hand over his. The tears were waiting, but at this moment she needed to be strong for him.

"Tony?" she smiled. "We're going to be O.K."

Stark tried to speak, but there was only a faint whisper. She could see the love in his eyes.

"You can rest now," she said.

And the whisper stopped, his eyes closed, and his hand fell away from hers. Tony Stark—Iron Man—was dead.

**Thanos watched as the remains of his armies became dust.**

## *The Final Chapter*

The sun is shining as the spaceship lands on Clint Barton's farm. Lila and her brothers rush to him. He holds them tightly. He looks at the tree with the target and remembers his fear when he first saw the empty spaces where his children had been. It was a different world. A world that he helped to change—and that Natasha gave her life for.

The farm is quiet, but it is not silent. He is not alone now.

He sees Laura, and his heart melts again. Another empty space filled.

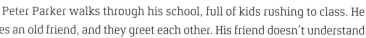

Peter Parker walks through his school, full of kids rushing to class. He sees an old friend, and they greet each other. His friend doesn't understand why it is a special meeting. Peter does.

In Wakanda, T'Challa, Shuri, and their mother look out over their city, which is full of light and life again.

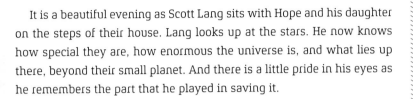

It is a beautiful evening as Scott Lang sits with Hope and his daughter on the steps of their house. Lang looks up at the stars. He now knows how special they are, how enormous the universe is, and what lies up there, beyond their small planet. And there is a little pride in his eyes as he remembers the part that he played in saving it.

"Everybody wants a happy ending." It is Stark's voice, speaking to a group of friends and family through a hologram. "But it doesn't always happen. Maybe this time." He smiles, relaxed, a slightly faded copy of himself sitting on a chair. "I'm hoping that if you play this back, it's in celebration."

There is a pause. Perhaps he is remembering the last message that he recorded for Pepper—on the Guardians of the Galaxy's spaceship.

"What a world." Stark shakes his head. "What a universe. The forces of darkness and light that have gathered. For better or worse, that's the reality that Morgan's going to have to find a way to grow up in. So, I thought I'd better record this greeting ... you know, in case I die. This time travel that we're going to try tomorrow ... I'm not sure we can survive it. But that's the risk that heroes take, right?" Then, his voice gets more cheerful. "Hey—everything's going to work exactly as it's supposed to."

He smiles and crosses to his old helmet, whose recording device is playing back his words. He looks directly into the camera, and into Morgan's eyes. "I love you three thousand," he says softly. And he flicks off the message.

Avengers and friends, heroes from every part of Stark's full life, stand quietly, as a circle of flowers with his name on it drifts across the lake. There are old people and young people, friends from Earth and from beyond; people of all ages, all colors, with different strengths and weaknesses, and with different memories of the love and power of this one man, who had brought them all together. Each face is pale and respectful. There are tears.

Barton thinks of Natasha. "I would really like to be able to tell her," he says to Wanda, "that we won."

Wanda stares out over the water. The memory of Vision, her love, who died when Thanos pulled the Mind Stone from his head, will always be with her.

"She knows. They both do," she says.

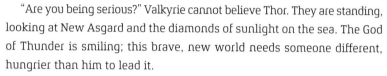

"Are you being serious?" Valkyrie cannot believe Thor. They are standing, looking at New Asgard and the diamonds of sunlight on the sea. The God of Thunder is smiling; this brave, new world needs someone different, hungrier than him to lead it.

"It's time for me to be who I *am* and not who I'm *supposed* to be," he tells her. Valkyrie will lead their people—the surviving Asgardians—differently perhaps, but well. "And I ..." He looks at the Guardians' spaceship, waiting a short walk away. Excitement rises in his chest. "For the first time in a thousand years, I have no path. I do have a ride, though."

"Use it or lose it!" Rocket says impatiently.

**"For the first time in a thousand years, I have no path. I do have a ride, though."**

Peter Quill's thoughts are, as always, with Gamora—where she is, what happened to her, why she disappeared? He knows that he will search until he finds her again.

His dreams are interrupted by the big man with blond hair and a deep voice who sits beside him at the controls, like a boy in a toy racing car.

"Ah!" Thor smiles broadly. "The Asgardians of the Galaxy are back together again! Now, where to first?"

He touches the map on the screen and chooses a destination.

"Hey!" Quill says. "This is *my* ship. *I'm* the leader here."

"Of course." Thor smiles again. "I know—of course you are, Quail."

"*Quail?*" Quill lifts his chin. "It's *Quill* ... and when you touch the map, I think you don't realize that I'm the leader here."

"You should fight for the honor of leading us!" Drax suggested.

"That sounds fair," Nebula agreed.

"Use knives!" Mantis said enthusiastically.

"No need," Thor smiled. "Everyone knows who the leader is."

"Yes, me." Quill looks at Thor. "Right?"

Steve Rogers steps onto the new Quantum Tunnel platform that Hulk has built near the lake. In one hand, he carries a special box containing all six Infinity Stones; in the other, he holds Thor's hammer.

"You know they have to go back to the exact moment we got them," Hulk reminds him.

"Yeah, I know," Captain America agrees. "We have to keep their futures the same."

Sam Wilson and Bucky Barnes watch him pull back his shoulders and lift his chin.

"How long is this going to take?" Wilson asks Hulk.

"For him—as long as he needs. For us—five seconds." Hulk flicks the switches.

"Going quantum, in three–two–one!" There is a bright flash, and Rogers is gone. The watchers hold their breath. "And returning ..." Hulk flicks another switch, "in five–four–three–two–one ..."

The platform remains empty.

"What!" Wilson cries. "Where is he? Get him back!"

"I don't know! I'm ..."

"Sam!" Bucky is looking toward the lake. Hulk and Wilson join him. There, sitting staring out at the water, is the figure of a man.

Slowly, Wilson walks down to the lake. "Cap?"

The man turns, and a smile plays on his lips. It is Rogers. But this Rogers is different from the brave, young Avenger who stepped onto the platform a short time ago. This Rogers is an old man. His hair is gray, and his shoulders have dropped. But the eyes are the same bright blue, and the lines on his face are from a life happily lived.

Wilson smiles, too. "So," he asks, "did something go wrong—or did something go right?"

"Well, after I put the Stones back, I thought about getting some of that life that Tony was always telling me to get. So, I did." Rogers's voice is soft, and gentler than Wilson has ever known it. The old man's eyes half-close with the memory. "It was ... beautiful," he says.

"I can't imagine living in a world without Captain America," Wilson says sadly.

Rogers reaches for something at his feet. He passes the Captain America shield to his old friend. "Try it on."

Wilson can't hide his shock. Can he really do this? "I'll do my best," he says quietly.

"That's why it's yours." Rogers holds his friend's hands, and Wilson sees the gold wedding ring on his finger.

Music is playing. The young couple that are dancing in the room have their arms tightly around each other as they move softly to the music. Their eyes are closed. The woman smiles gently, and the man feels her smile. He opens his eyes, and they look lovingly at each other. Then, Steve Rogers leans forward and kisses the one love of his whole life—Peggy Carter. The five seconds in the Quantum Tunnel have given him a lifetime to love her again.

He opens his eyes, and they look lovingly at each other.

# Activities

## Chapters 1–2

### Before you read

**1** Look at the Word List at the back of the book. Check the meanings of new words. Then name:

**a** a game or sport that uses a *target*
**b** a job for which you need to wear a *helmet*
**c** your favorite *device*
**d** an occasion when you might *tremble*
**e** another animal that can *roar*
**f** something that you think is *inevitable* in the future
**g** a person who might use an *ax* for his or her job
**h** a *super* hero

**2** Look at Who's Who? Discuss these questions with another student.

**a** Read about the characters. Which one has the most interesting superpower, in your opinion? Why do you think this?
**b** Now look at the pictures in Chapters 1 and 2. How many of the characters can you name? Discuss what you know about them.

**3** Read the Introduction and answer these questions.

**a** Which Infinity Stone would you most like to possess? What would you do with it? Why?
**b** Have you seen any of the movies mentioned? If you have, which is your favorite? If not, which would you like to see? Why?
**c** What happened at the end of *Avengers: Infinity War*? What was Thanos's plan? Did he succeed?
**d** What problems can overpopulation cause on Earth?
**e** After the battles of *Avengers: Infinity War*, where might we find the surviving characters at the beginning of *Avengers: Endgame*? How do they feel and what are they doing, do you think?

## While You Read

**4**   Answer the questions.

    **a** What are these people doing at the start of the story?

      Lila: _____

      Clint: _____

      Lila's brothers: _____

      Clint's wife: _____

    **b** What frightens Barton at the end of Chapter 1?

    _____

**5**   Complete the sentences with the correct names.

    **a** _____ has helped Stark recover on the Guardians of the Galaxy's spaceship.

    **b** Stark records a message for _____ .

    **c** _____ brings the spaceship to the Avengers building on Earth.

    **d** Stark is sad because he could not save _____ .

    **e** _____ pilots the spaceship to find Thanos.

    **f** _____ has destroyed the Infinity Stones.

    **g** _____ kills Thanos with his ax.

## After you read

**6**   Work in pairs. Imagine you are one of these characters. Describe what you did and what happened to you in Chapter 1 or 2.

    *Clint Barton*    *Tony Stark*    *Steve Rogers*
    *Thanos*    *Thor*    *Carol Danvers*

**7**   Work with another student. Have this conversation between Stark and Natasha after the travelers return from the Garden, Thanos's new home.

    *Student A:* You are Stark. Ask Natasha about the Stones. Did they get them? Can they use them to return the disappeared? How do you react to Natasha's information?

    *Student B:* You are Natasha. Explain what happened on the Garden planet and why.

# Chapters 3-4

## Before you read

**8** Complete these sentences with words from the Word List at the back of the book.

**a** The bomb exploded, but everyone was lucky and they all … .
**b** People wear sunglasses to … their eyes from too much sunlight.
**c** I often lose my phone signal when a train goes through a … .
**d** There was a sudden … of electricity, and all the lights went off.
**e** The … of the music was a house down the road, where they were having a party.
**f** In a daring jewelry … last year, the thieves took rings worth millions of dollars.

**9** What do you think the Avengers will do next? Choose a possibility and explain why.

**a** They will start thinking about a plan to bring back the disappeared.
**b** They will continue as a group, doing routine jobs.
**c** They will split up and go their different ways.

## While you read

**10** Write the speaker's name.

**a** "We have to take brave, baby steps." ............................................
**b** "You're so big!" ............................................
**c** "Now we smell like garbage." ............................................
**d** "There's a part of me that doesn't even want to find him." ............................................
**e** "And I was better because of it." ............................................
**f** "Are you talking about a time machine?" ............................................

Discuss what he or she is talking about in each case.

**11** Circle the words that are wrong and write the correct words.

**a** Stark is happy to get a visit from his friends. ............................................
**b** Stark thinks that Lang's idea is excellent. ............................................
**c** Banner is stuck in Hulk's body by accident. ............................................
**d** Stark changes his opinion of the time travel plan when he remembers his wife. ............................................

**e** The time travel test goes well. ............................................

**f** Stark goes to the Avengers building to tell them that time travel is not possible. ............................................

**Now explain the sentences.**

## After you read

**12** Work with another student. Have this conversation.

*Student A*: You are Rogers. You run a group that helps survivors of the Blip. Listen and give advice.
*Student B*: You lost your family in the Blip. How has life changed for you? What have you been doing? How do you feel now? Tell Rogers.

**13** Imagine another hologram group meeting between Natasha and the other Avengers who are working. List problems that the group might discuss.

# Chapters 5–6

## Before you read

**14** Discuss these questions.

**a** Who do you think will be members of the time travel team?
**b** What problems might there be in a plan that involves time travel to change Thanos's actions?
**c** What kind of lives do you think Thor and Clint Barton are leading now?

## While you read

**15** What happens next? Write the next sentences in your notebook.

**a** Hulk gets on the Guardians' spaceship with Rocket.
**b** Barton kills a gang leader on a Tokyo street.
**c** Barton finds himself back on his farm.
**d** Rogers asks Thor to talk about the Reality Stone.
**e** Rogers can't see how the team can get all the Stones.

**16** Write the answers to these questions in your notebook.

   **a** Which Avengers go to which times and places in the past to find which Infinity Stones?

   **b** What is happening in New York when Avengers 2023 arrive?

   **c** Who is guarding the Time Stone in 2012?

   **d** How does Thanos learn about the Avengers' plan?

   **e** Who does Captain America 2023 come face to face with on a glass bridge?

### After you read

**17** Work in pairs. You are on the street in Tokyo and see the fight between an American (Clint Barton) and another man. Report it to a Japanese police officer, who will ask you questions.

**18** Read Chapter 6 again. Discuss how you think these people are feeling at the end of the chapter:

*Captain America 2023    Iron Man 2023    Gamora    Thanos*

# Chapters 7–8

### Before you read

**19** Discuss these questions. What do you think?

   **a** What will Stark's next plan be, after losing the Tesseract?

   **b** How will the fight between the two Captain Americas end?

   **c** How can Hulk persuade the Ancient One to give him the Time Stone?

   **d** How can Thanos use Nebula 2023 to help him?

   **e** Someone will die in the next part of the book. Who—and why?

### While you read

**20** Write answers to these questions in your notebook.

   **a** What two things shock Captain America 2012 and stop him fighting for a moment?

   **b** Why does the Ancient One not want to give the Time Stone to Hulk?

**c** What does Thanos learn from Nebula 2014's brain?
**d** Why is Thor very happy when they leave Asgard?
**e** Why does Ebony Maw want to kill Nebula 2014?

**21** Write the correct names or places.

    **a** ................................................ gets angry with Iron Man because he doesn't have enough particles to get all the Stones.

    **b** Stark and Rogers go to an ................................................ (1970) to find the Tesseract again.

    **c** ................................................ finds the Tesseract.

    **d** Stark meets ................................................ while he is in 1970.

    **e** ................................................ finds more Pym Particles.

    **f** Rogers sees ................................................ while he is in 1970.

    **g** ................................................ dies in exchange for the Soul Stone.

## After you read

**22** Imagine that you are Clint Barton. Describe what happened on Vormir.

**23** Work with another student. Choose two of the Infinity Stones. What do you know about those Stones? Discuss where each Stone was and with whom at different times. Where are they now?

# Chapters 9–10

## Before you read

**24** Which one of these events do you think will happen in the next two chapters?

    **a** An Avenger goes back to Vormir to find Natasha.
    **b** Thor uses the gauntlet.
    **c** Thanos destroys the Avengers building.
    **d** Rocket is badly wounded in an explosion.
    **e** Thanos breaks Stormbreaker, Mjolnir, and Captain America's shield.

## While you read

**25** Who or what do the words in *italics* refer to?

    **a** "Did we get *them* all?" ......................................

    **b** "Let *me* just do this one thing right. Please!" ......................................

    **c** "And *you're* not in the best physical shape." ......................................

    **d** "I can't hold *it* much longer." ......................................

    **e** "*I*'m down here, too. *I*'m coming." ......................................

    **f** "*I* will try to kill you … Many times." ......................................

    **g** "Together, *we* can stop *him*." ......................................

**26** What are these characters talking or thinking about? Write answers in your notebook.

    **a** "I don't much care." (Stark)

    **b** "You have shown me that I was wrong." (Thanos)

    **c** Was he seeing double? (Hawkeye)

    **d** There was another person in the world who was worthy. (Thor)

    **e** "On your left!" (Falcon)

    **f** "Avengers, assemble!" (Captain America)

## After you read

**27** Imagine you are one of these characters. Describe what happened to you in Chapters 9 and 10.

    *Nebula 2014*    *Hawkeye*    *Hulk*    *Captain America*

**28** Work with another student. With details from your imagination, describe Ant-Man's rescue of Rocket, War Machine, and Hulk.

# Chapters 11–12

## Before you read

**29** Discuss these questions.

    **a** What do you think will happen in the "endgame"?

    **b** One person uses the Pym Particles for a final journey. Why? Who will it be? What will happen to him or her?

## While you read

**30** In which order do these characters hold and/or carry the Infinity Stones during the battle? Write the numbers 1–6.

**a** Captain Marvel ............   **d** Thanos ............

**b** Iron Man ............   **e** Spider-Man ............

**c** Hawkeye ............   **f** Black Panther ............

**31** Answer the questions.

**a** How does Thor surprise Valkyrie?

**b** What are Thor's plans now?

**c** What do Thor and Quill argue about?

**d** Why does Rogers need to return to the past?

**e** How has Rogers changed when he returns? Why?

**f** What responsibility does Rogers pass to Wilson?

## After you read

**32** Discuss these questions with another student.

**a** How do these people change during the story?

*Clint Barton    Thor    Tony Stark*

**b** Thanos had a plan to solve the problem of overpopulation in the world. Do you think overpopulation really is a problem? Why (not)? If it is, what can we do to prevent or deal with it?

**33** Imagine that you could go back in time and meet yourself eight years ago. What would you say to your younger self? Tell another student.

# Writing

**34** Explain how the "disappeared" were returned to life.

**35** Choose a character from the story and imagine what he or she does the day after the story ends. Write a diary page for that day.

**36** Write about the life of either Tony Stark or Natasha Romanoff for an online newspaper after his or her death. Use the internet to find out more about their backgrounds.

**37** Imagine that there is another Infinity Stone. Write about it. What color is it? Where can it be found? What can it do? How can it be used for good or evil?

**38** Write a menu for a day's meals for Hulk. Think about breakfast, lunch, dinner, and snacks.

**39** Choose one of the Infinity Stones that Rogers had to return to the past. Write his report for the U.S. government of how he did this.

**40** Write the paragraphs that three people at Tony Stark's funeral added to a remembrance book.

**41** Write a conversation between the aging Steve Rogers and a friend, in which Rogers explains how five seconds in the Quantum Tunnel gave him a lifetime to love Peggy.

**42** Write about the story for a magazine. Would you recommend that other people read it?

**43** Plan the next movie for the remaining Avengers. Think about the title, the story, and the music. Write the opening scene.

# Word List

**arrow (n)** a thin, straight stick with a point that you can shoot as a sport or as a weapon

**assemble (v)** to gather together for a particular reason

**atom (n)** the tiniest part of a solid, liquid, or gas. **Subatomic** describes something that is smaller than an atom or that happens inside an atom.

**ax (n)** a tool used for cutting wood, usually with a steel edge, sometimes used as a weapon

**blast (n/v)** a strong wave of air or power that can destroy things. In this story, **blasters** are weapons.

**bow (n)** a piece of bent wood with string between its ends, used for shooting arrows

**crush (v)** to destroy something by stepping on it or putting something heavy on it; to shock someone greatly

**destruction (n)** the act of destroying something

**device (n)** a piece of electrical or mechanical equipment with a special use

**drift (v)** to be carried slowly by water or air. If you **drift off**, you fall asleep gradually.

**fade (v)** to slowly grow faint and disappear

**flick (n/v)** a sudden, quick movement

**gauntlet (n)** a thick, heavy glove

**heist (n)** a robbery, or theft of something very valuable

**helmet (n)** something that covers and protects the head during a sport or a fight

**hologram (n)** a special type of photograph that looks real, not flat, created using the science of **holography**

**inevitable (adj)** cannot be avoided, so is definitely going to happen

**leap (v)** to jump quickly and very high

**portal (n)** in this story, a gateway—created by magic or science—into another space or time

**pulse (n/v)** a strong, regular beat; for example, the beat that we can feel on our wrist as our blood moves around our body

**roar (n/v)** a very loud, deep noise, like the call of a lion

**rumble (n/v)** a continuous, deep sound, like thunder

**scepter (n)** a special and often beautiful stick that represents the power of the king or queen who carries it

**shield (n/v)** a wide piece of metal or other strong material used by police or fighters to protect themselves from attack

**snap (n/v)** the short, sharp noise made by moving one of your fingers quickly against your thumb

**sorcerer (n)** a person in stories who has magic powers

**source (n)** the place, thing, activity, or person that something comes from

**still (adj)** quiet and calm, not moving

**stun (v)** to surprise someone so greatly that he or she can't react; to make someone unconscious for a short time

**super (prefix/adj)** in this story, more or very powerful

**surge (n/v)** a sudden, powerful movement forward or upward

**survive (v)** to live after nearly dying

**target (n)** something that you aim to hit or find

**tremble (v)** to shake slightly and uncontrollably, especially because you are anxious or frightened

**tunnel (n)** an underground passage, often built through a hill or under a river

**worthy (adj)** deserving respect or a particular honor